DID I WRITE THAT OUT LOUD?

WE MIGHT AS WELL LAUGH, IT'S ONLY LIFE

By

Larry Ratliff

Anita,

All the best,

Larry Ratliff

DEDICATION

To Suellen, my loving wife and muse, and to my Mom and Dad, who never gave up on me, even though there were plenty of chances.

CONTENTS

ACKNOWLEDGMENTS

Thanks to Suellen, for encouraging me to write this book, to my friends for their support, to all the movie stars I've interviewed over the years and to life itself, for providing a heck of a roller coaster ride.

I HATE PANTS

C all it a gut feeling, but I'm pretty sure my pants are tightening up on purpose.

And there's something I need to get off my chest right now, although that hardly seems to be the correct body part.

I hate pants.

I've tried to embrace them, to forgive and forget when they shrink unexpectedly or change colors or, worst of all, bully all their wash-cycle pals into adopting their color of choice.

Since I'm no longer able to hide my discontent, let's just get it out there. Slacks, trousers, jeans: Call them what you like. I hate pants.

And they obviously loathe me.

I've never taken a deep breath and zipped or buttoned up what I can honestly call a comfortable pair of pants, for instance.

The problem isn't just in my jeans, it's in my genes.

Both of my grandfathers had what I now look back on as pants issues. And that was way before Blue Bell.

Wally, on my father's side of the jean pool, opted for the below-the-belly approach. When he passed away, Wally still proudly sported the same size pants he wore as a teenager. Of course he could only comfortably get them up slightly above his knees.

Pa, my grandfather on my mother's side, gave up the pants struggle altogether in his later years. He chose the very loose fitting trouser. They were held up by suspenders and a grim determination to squelch the evil pants demons by simply avoiding the confrontation.

I choose to stand and fight. Or at least lie back on the bed, take a deep breath that sounds like a coyote howl, and fight. I will position my pants where they belong so, ugh, help me.

But it hasn't been easy. Right now I'm in the middle of a major pants crisis. The one pair of blue jeans I own that can almost be called semi-comfortable recently turned on me.

I don't know how long trouble's been brewing. But my jeans are definitely in cahoots with the plumbing at my apartment.

If, like me, you never venture near the "slim" slacks area of any store for fear of being laughed back to the "hefty" zone, you know what I mean when I say I take the chore of washing jeans very seriously.

The wash cycle is cold-cold for anything that adorns, or is stretched to ungodly proportions over the lower portion of my body. Obviously, the dryer is only a dangerous, sneering bystander.

About a month ago, a pant-plumbing alliance found a way around my tedious attempts to keep the jeans the size they were in the beginning (when we got along OK).

Somewhere during the cold-cold wash and rinse cycle, the plumbing universe in my apartment decided to defy logic, physics and my pleas to hold the line on shrinkage.

You turn on the cold water tap at my place and you get very warm – almost hot – water. While this is a good thing if one is in too much of a hurry to wait until a pill leaves the front lips to dissolve, generally it stinks.

There's another problem. Call me silly, but since I already have a hot water tap, I would prefer for cold water to splash out of its designated pipe.

Eventually the hot water backs off and becomes just lukewarm. And, if you hang around long enough, somewhat cool. Cold, I'm afraid, is no longer in the picture.

One of the pluses of apartment living is being able to delegate problems to someone else when pesky things like this pop up. (Actually, that's the only good thing about sharing a ceiling and wall with strangers.)

The baffled facial expressions and responses like, "Dude, I've never heard that one before" are amusing, all right. And they do momentarily take my mind off the painful cinch around my midsection. But so far nothing has been done to win the cold war.

Why not just buy bigger pants?

That would just play into the hands of the trouser conspirators, my friend. I should have known from the moment I headed off to first grade, accompanied by the irritating sound of stiffly starched Levi legs shuffling and scraping together that this would be a lifelong battle.

Pants just rub me the wrong way. (Sometimes a little baby powder helps.)

Some of the words I've hated most during my lifetime have come from trouser entanglements. Words like "husky," "relaxed fit" (That's a crock) and "big man."

In fact, the only word I've ever loved that even vaguely has anything to do with lower body attire is "sweatpants."

Now that's a word every stomach-challenged person can really get into. If sweatpants ever become acceptable in anything other than sit-around-the-house-and-watch-football circles, I might just venture out of the house again.

Pants are such a waist. I need a tepid shower.

PUTTING A LID ON
THE JALAPEÑO JAR

*I*t took me 15 years to discover I had no talent for writing, but I couldn't give it up because by that time I was too famous. -- Robert Benchley

On Sept. 8, 2011, I wrote:

This is a difficult day. This is the day I put a lid on the jalapeño jar, so to speak.

At least for now, I have written my final film review and dished out my last batch of jalapeños via my hot-or-not movie rating system.

A colleague heard the news and responded that he could understand being out of creative gas after writing thousands of film reviews from 1980 to last week.

That's kind, but not the reason.

In what some will describe as a bold move and others will, I'm sure, dub a dumb one, I'm redirecting my career as a film critic.

While there are hundreds, perhaps thousands of people in this country calling themselves film critics these days -- and maybe two or three dozen actually qualified -- the fact is the field is more crowded than a stadium overflowing with starry-eyed warblers clamoring to become the next "American Idol."

From this moment on, I'll be concentrating on Movie Memories with Larry Ratliff, my classic movie lecture/presentation series, which has taken off quite nicely but requires much of my time.

Once again, I'm taking the road less traveled. Just like I did in 1980 when I became a film critic in the first place.

It's funny how the mind works, or doesn't. I can remember with vivid clarity my first professional movie review. It was published in the *Valley Morning Star,* a daily newspaper in Harlingen, Texas, over the Fourth of July weekend in 1980.

As you can imagine, there were no critic screenings back then in a modest-sized South Texas town. After taking a job in the newspaper's sports department with a semi-hidden agenda to become a film critic, I finally convinced the editor to let me write a movie review after some badgering.

I hurried over to the local movie house to see the big movie debuting that weekend. It turned out to be "Airplane!" the outrageous spoof comedy.

Clear and succinct in my mind, that seems like yesterday. I have reviewed countless movies since, running the gamut from dreadful to soul-stirring brilliant. I was even fortunate enough to win some awards doing a task from the heart that I loved.

The jalapeño jar may be closed with the lid tightened, but I have not sealed it with wax like my mother used to do to preserve her jars of pickles and tomatoes.

A wise man -- I think it was Sean Connery -- once said, "Never say never."

Since I may change my mind at some point, I'm leaving the jalapeño jar slightly ajar, if you'll forgive the pun.

I know you will forgive the pun.

You always have, and I'll be forever grateful for that.

I'M NOT TAKING STAND-UP COMEDY SITTING DOWN

Making an announcement like this on April Fools' Day (2013) probably says more about my comic t-t-timing, or semi-lack of same, than a sane man would normally care to share. But here goes.

I'm adding stand-up comedy -- a lifelong love of mine -- to my repertoire of Movie Memories presentations.

You should know I've made a fool of myself as a stand-up comedian before. So this decision does not come without precedent. It just arrives without the benefit of clear thinking.

Welcome to "We Might As Well Laugh," an hour-long comic look at the world around us. I'll talk about things that bug me, like tiny print on medicine bottles, hearing aids that whisper in our ears when we least expect it and a world divided equally but uneasily between the two titans, mayo and Miracle Whip.

It is now officially OK to laugh at me, laugh with me and, perhaps, chuckle a little at yourselves as well. After all, many of us are navigating uncharted life beyond 50 or 60, which is the new 50 and the old ... What? I've lost my train of thought again.

Oh yeah. Seniors deserve fun, too. After all, these are trying times. Meteors and asteroids are buzzing Mother Earth. Sinkholes are swallowing up houses and golfers (If you're keeping score, that's a sinkhole in one or one in sinkhole) and now giant monster mosquitoes are buzzing around Florida like Mothra. Yeah, huh.

Thus the title: "We Might As Well Laugh."

So, join the comedy-for-seniors rebellion with me, won't you? Book your group, club or facility today for some real fun that we can all identify with.

We'll laugh 'til it hurts, which won't take long for those of us with joint ailments. Let's have some fun with comedy only those 45 or 50 or with even more life experience can truly appreciate (and guffaw at).

And let's not forget that some of us remain plenty rebellious. Young people think it's hip to wear their pants way down low, for instance. That's way south of hip (or hips), if you ask me.

Perhaps in an effort to balance the universe, some senior men appear to be raising the waistline to mid-chest. Have you seen Clint Eastwood lately?

And speaking of seniors, do we really have to refer to ourselves in high school terms? As far as I can tell, there's no big homecoming game and dance looming and no senior prom coming up.

We've got something better: Memories; movie and otherwise.

You know what? I'm not taking stand-up comedy sitting down. Give me a second to get up. O-o-o-kay, I'm up.

We might as well laugh.

LIFE'S FUNNY OUTTAKES

Don't be too quick to jump out of your seat and head for the catered buffet after my funeral.

You'll want to hang around for my life's funny outtakes. You know, like we see at the end of Jackie Chan movies. The kung-fuey master misses his mark during a stunt and mangles a body part.

"Ha, ha, poor Jackie. Better him than me. Where shall we eat?"

Life should be more like the movies, especially when it comes to matters of love, lust and loss. That way love really would mean never having to say you're sorry.

And when we're backed into the corner of absolute guilt, there'd always be Rhett Butler's breezy "Gone With the Wind" comeback, "Frankly, (insert innocent party's name here), I just don't give a ding-dang-darn."

So why not our own funny outtakes after the serious business of a life lived is in the books? I'd rather send 'em home chuckling than saying things like: "Didn't he look natural? I mean, he always wore way too much makeup and combed his hair sideways like that."

Or, "Too bad they never stopped the world so Larry could get on." Or, "Did that potato salad taste weird to you?"

So here lies my life's funny outtakes. File them away in your memory bank until, you know, until …

Second grade: I didn't think talking back to the teacher was so bad (probably the first hint of my rebellious struggle with authority). But I got sent to the principal's office for a paddling anyway.

During the long walk down the dusty hall I came up with a brilliant plan to avoid corporal punishment and yet please my authoritarian teacher. I bypassed the principal's office completely and went instead into the restroom. I splashed water on my face like I'd been crying.

When I returned to my classroom (slouching, head down, turning in what I believed to be an Oscar-worthy-yet-pouty performance), I looked up. The principal was sitting in my desk.

That did not end well.

Fourth grade: Instead of paying attention much of the time, I'd draw World War II enemy fighter planes (a formation of dreaded Japanese Zeros) on a piece of paper and attack them under my desk in the name of the Allied Forces and all that's good.

I didn't pretend to be a crack shot, so I turned the piece of paper over on my leg and attacked with determined vigor with the pointy end of my drawing compass.

As far as I know, I'm the only fourth grader ever wounded in a foreign war.

Thirteenth grade: An older fellow grocery store employee landed a six-pack. It was my first experience drinking warm beer (or any beer, for that matter). After a couple of hours cruising the streets looking for girls who could appreciate the beer swilling qualities of a young man such as myself, I had to, you know, go.

My friend, who in retrospect might not have been the finest source of sage advice, pulled the car over to the curb and assured me that everything would be fine.

And it was for about 20 seconds. That's when I noticed the flashing red lights and heard the stern, "What do you think you're doing, young man?"

I still contend it was a tad harsh for the officer to tell me to get out of Arlington and never come back.

Remember my hang-up about authority figures? I've been back to the mid-city hamlet three or four times in the last 35 years. Take that, Mr. Can't Wee-Wee In My Town.

Usually, though, I just go around. I don't want trouble.

The forty-fifth grade: Long story short, I was way too busy with my career to be around on moving day. My wife Suellen took care of everything with the help of some friends. I left town on Friday morning. When I returned Sunday night, it was to a new address.

Naturally, when she picked me up at the airport we wanted to celebrate our new home over nachos and a top-shelf margarita or two, or "Two more, beer-tender!"

We were giggling, a little goofy and making too much late-night noise as we poured out of the car in our new driveway. I remember Suellen saying, "Hey, I didn't put this potted plant here" as I jiggled the key in the lock with the fervor of a fourth grader attacking enemy aircraft with the bloody end of a drawing compass.

We scrambled back into the car and – just like in the movies – found the right house in Take 2.

Luckily, no police officer kicked us out of San Antonio and told us never to come back that night. After all, we only missed our house by one driveway.

BIG TEX: THE MOURNING AFTER

Before the sun even came up Saturday, Oct. 20 (2012), I was sitting in our darkened living room teary-eyed.

Yes, I'll admit it. I was on the brink of weeping over 6,000 pounds of charred steel, a super-plus-sized Dickies belt buckle weighing 50 pounds and two giant plastic hands that, upon being loaded onto a huge flatbed trailer, appeared to be signaling a definite "thumbs down."

It was all that remained of Big Tex.

The 52-foot-tall Santa-turned-giant cowpoke that welcomed folks to the Texas State Fair for 60 years with a friendly slow drawl ("How-dee f-o-l-k-s") burst into flames shortly after 10 Friday morning, perhaps spooking The World's Smallest Horse (also a State Fair perennial) as he sipped a teaspoon of water just off the Midway.

We can only hope it didn't melt the life-sized butter sculpture of Girl Scouts chillin' in the Creative Arts Building.

Even though the fire -- thought to be electrical -- may have started somewhere in Big Tex's size 70 boots that stand -- excuse me, stood -- over 7-feet tall, smoke followed by flames first billowed out from under the tall cowpoke's collar.

I know a little about being hot under the collar. Just ask my wife about the guy a few blocks away who thought we were stalking his house the other day when we were out walking the dog.

And I can eerily relate, at least somewhat, to what Tex went through. I, too, was fired once on a Friday. A little after 10 a.m. it was, in fact. And though no one will ever admit it, my untimely exit also probably had something to do with being slightly north of the big 6-0.

The only real difference between Big Tex and me is that the long, really tall Texan kept standing, even as his face melted and turned to ash. I, on the other hand, was crushed. (Just for the record, I prefer being fired in person. Over the telephone takes some of the fun out of it.)

Oh I suppose there are other differences between Big Tex and me. Tex's belt, when there was a belt, measured 23 feet long. At times mine feels just short of that; I'm guessing about 21-feet, 11 inches. (Damn those "10 pints of Blue Bell ice cream" sales at competing grocery stores.)

Why was I on the brink of shedding tears over a goofy-looking Santa/cowboy?

Big Tex was my friend. That's why. He was always there for me. And he never laughed at me, although there were plenty of opportunities.

When I was about 13 and in junior high around 1960, I eagerly awaited my first unchaperoned trip to the Fair. I had foolishly arranged four or five first "dates" with unsuspecting Grand Prairie schoolgirls.

I told each of them to meet me at Big Tex. Perhaps inspired by Dr Pepper, I meticulously planned to meet the first one at 10, then 2, then 4. You get the idea. Come to think of it, I may have invented speed dating.

After an hour and a half or so of riding and almost hurling on the Tilt-A-Whirl, throwing darts and missing balloons and tossing all my best lines at my date-o'-the-moment, I would excuse myself and head back to good ol' Big Tex for the next brief encounter.

My plan went bad, of course. Somewhere on the Midway in mid-afternoon, my jilted 10 a.m. saw me with my 2 o'clock. She didn't say anything. But after we passed, I looked back to see the "young woman scorned" ripping (with a fury I had no idea existed) the stitched "Larry" out of the sailor cap I bought her only a short time earlier.

And just two or three years ago, I exhibited more bad State Fair judgment. My wife Suellen even warned me about wearing brand new, lily white tennis shoes (sneakers for all you folks north of Lake Texoma) to the Fair.

What could possibly go wrong, I pondered. Well, this. After tiptoeing carefully across the fairgrounds to say a mental "howdy" to Big Tex, we bought steaming, fresh-out-of-the-grease corny dogs at the Fletcher's stand just a few feet from Tex's boots.

It only took about 15 seconds for a huge glob of mustard to drip off my corny dog and splatter onto my formerly all-white left shoe. Not just on it, you understand, but soaking throughout the laces.

Once again, the big cowpoke didn't judge. Big Tex just grinned that familiar, all-knowing goofy smile.

I reacted differently. It burned me up.

Sorry. No offense, big guy.

Looking forward to seeing the new you next year.

ONE FLU OVER THE CUCKOO'S NEST

S ong sung to the tune of "One for My Baby":

"It's a quarter to three,

There's no one in the place 'cept you and me

So stick 'em up Joe"

Actually, it's a quarter to 4 a.m. when I wake up in a flu-induced fog.

It's not yet morning; in fact hours from it.

But not really nighttime, either.

So my dilemma: Do I slug another shot of NyQuil, or is it close enough to groggy dawn for DayQuil, an awful orange liquid that tastes like 30 ml of kick-boxing-induced sweat made semi-swallowable by Sweet'N Low, or "the pink one" as a flight attendant referred to it the other day?

I have the flu, but not THE FLU. You know, the dreaded, highly contagious swine flu.

The swine flu is no laughing matter south of the border, and perhaps soon in the U.S. People are dying by the score in Mexico.

In fact it's so bad that the drug lords are forced to wear medical masks over their bandannas when they execute the innocent. And they're rethinking those shallow graves.

I don't expect to expire from this, although it would set up the tombstone epitaph I've threatened to put on my "last wish" list in my more cynical, neglected moments:

"Here lies Larry

Told you I was sick"

I can't get no sympathy for my (body) aches and pains. I probably deserve that. Don't know why but too sick to ponder about it long.

Maybe if I dry-cough a little louder. No sympathy help there. Still told to find the thermometer myself if I want my temperature checked. That's all right. The stupid thing doesn't work anyway. It's about as reliable as the home-park radar gun at the new Yankee Stadium. Damn Yankees; my throat hurts.

On my own, so I semi-walk slumped more than usual to the medicine cabinet for some relief. At this point, anything is welcome.

I push aside the Aleve ("Strength to last all day." Yeah, right), move over the thin box of generic non-drowsy allergy relief ("Compare to Claritin." I did, it sucks.) and feel slightly better because I can ignore, at least for now, the nauseating yellow, green and white Dulcolax Laxative box.

Finally, there it is. I found an unopened bottle of **3:45 a.m. Quil**!

Better check the warnings on the bottle first: "Ask a doctor before you use if you have liver disease, heart disease, thyroid disease, diabetes, high blood pressure, trouble urinating due to enlarged prostate gland, cough that occurs with too much phlegm (mucus), persistent or chronic cough as occurs with smoking, asthma or emphysema, or a sodium-restricted diet."

Have you ever tried to ask a doctor anything at 3:45 in the morning?

Besides, now it's 3:55. The 3:45 a.m.Quil is no longer what I need.

It's back to the medicine cabinet or perhaps my fitful dreams for what I really need:

My Mommy and a thermometer that works. In that order.

WHAT I DID ON MY
FALL(ING) VACATION

As long as I can remember, I've fought hard against the odds -- uphill, wind in my face, lacking necessary God-given talent tools and/or budget -- to be The Guy.

I longed to be the center of attention, the guy all eyes gravitated to first as a radio DJ, then as a TV news reporter/anchor, a stand-up comedian (let's not go there) and film critic, which actually worked out pretty well.

I finally reached that coveted center-stage point over the weekend in a tiny Texas coastal town.

But I never wanted to be this guy.

It's 4:30 in the morning. I'm coming out of a blackout fog on a cold condo bathroom floor with loved ones and a complete stranger staring down at me.

Holy crap! Is that a defibrillator?

But wait, let's flash back a little like they do in the movies.

My wife Suellen and I look forward with great anticipation to our rare chances to get away to the beach. We don't own a condo. We will, though, just as soon as our lottery numbers cooperate.

So we rent. And we love it. Last weekend's trip began like many of the others. Relatives and friends would join us at the beach. We would gather for coffee and chats in the morning, dig our toes into the sun-kissed sand during the day as the seagulls circled low overhead and toast the good life once the sun went down.

But we -- and when I say we I really mean I -- ventured, as they say in the movies, "off-script" this time. I've been dieting, as some of you and this region's perplexed Blue Bell ice cream distributor know.

My calorie count has been low (too low you are about to discover). And I've been pushing myself physically playing tennis (which I recently rediscovered that I really enjoy) in the hot sun without adequate hydration. Played a rousing game of "rediscover tennis" with the family that very morning, in fact.

Distill all that with a libation or two to celebrate good times, the moon shining brilliantly on the Gulf water and the fact that the Texas Rangers had clinched the American League West division championship earlier in the day and around 4:30 a.m. we get these buzzwords:

Cramp. LEG CRAMP! Now in both legs! "Ow, ow, ow, OW!"

"Got to get to the bathroom."

Splat.

(That's the sound of yours truly blacking out and collapsing in a clump on the living room floor; un-carpeted of course.)

Panic. (That would be Suellen as she comes to my rescue.)

In the bathroom now.

Splat again.

(My best description of collapse No. 2 brought back thoughts of the late Howard Cosell's call when George Foreman belted Joe Frazier to the mat in the first round of the 1973 world heavyweight boxing championship in Kingston, Jamaica: "Down goes Frazier! Down goes Frazier!")

Serious panic now.

(Suellen makes frantic call to daughter Lisa and son-in-law Johnny, who are two floors down.)

I'm up. Johnny, a medical research scientist working on a cure for cancer, slums a little and checks me out. He says my pulse is low.

"I think I'm fine now."

Splat -- the trifecta.

Now we're back to real time. The paramedics have arrived.

Actually it's just one paramedic, a nice young lady with slurred speech. I'm told later she must have recently gotten her tongue pierced. Presumably, it was on purpose.

"My partner's downthairs throwing up," she casually announces.

Still, she does a very capable job of hooking up my EKG, checking my pulse (Yep, low) and pricking my finger for blood to check the glucose level (low there as well). The good news: I do not require the defibrillator.

Suddenly, two more paramedics appear. One of the new arrivals, whose partner is not downstairs tossing his cookies or jumbo fried shrimp or whatever, appears extremely professional and caring. Still that makes three paramedics. I think the odd number is somehow throwing the universe off-kilter. At least it is mine.

"Sorry, guys," I tell them, "You're not meeting me on my best day."

"We rarely meet people on their best days," the professional appearing one responds with rather exceptional comic timing.

Full disclosure: I'm kidding around with them to keep from being scared out of my wits. When it's generally decided that I don't appear to be in immediate serious danger and can avoid taking a ride in their ambulance (with the puking guy driving), I relax a little.

"Your color ish coming back," the emergency responder with the trendy spike in her tongue says.

"That's good," I respond.

But I can't resist:

"What color am I?"

SEE, I'M NO GOOD WITHOUT YOU

A ttention U.S. citizens who are 65, about to turn 65, who know someone who's 65 or have ever driven 65:

Your medical cares are over, or soon will be.

There's a little thing the United States of Us government has put into place called Medicare.

It's for hard working people like us who have worked all our lives -- paying into the government coffer -- to handle our ills once we are ... seniors. (There I said it: Seniors!)

Even if you've been without health insurance since the economy tanked and your benefits, extended benefits and way over-priced health insurance have lapsed, the U.S. of Us has your back and your front.

Just not your head.

That's why although I don't usually dedicate songs in a situation like this, I'm suggesting that you listen to the late, great Frank Sinatra sing "All of Me" before I explain how Medicare works, or, in my case, doesn't work.

All of me, why not take all of me

Can't you see I'm no good without you

Medicare, as explained in rather cryptic terms at http://www.medicare.gov/default.aspx on your friendly Internet, basically covers us from the neck down. If you have hearing difficulties, as I do, Medicare is out.

I SAID, MEDICARE CAN'T HELP YOU!

Need help seeing, as in Lasik eye surgery? Good news!

Nope, actually bad news. My bad. I was looking at the glass eye section of Medicare coverage. It's all a little blurry.

Your good-bye left me with eyes that cry

How can I get along without you

That brings us, if you'll excuse the expression, to the mouth:

Bridge over troubled molars

Take my lips I want to lose them

Take my arms I'll never use them

When I was a mere lad of 12, my mother -- a stay-at-home-mom -- ventured out of our Grand Prairie home to work in downtown Dallas as a keypunch-operator. The reason? To buy braces for my teeth so I'd have a full set of impressive choppers all my life. "All my life" being the key phrase.

I won't bother explaining what a keypunch operator was. If you've read this far (and you're tapping your toes to Frank Sinatra), you'll know what that was.

To make a long sad story short, I've got serious problems with two upper molars and Medicare doesn't care. Our Us government, you see, is only concerned about its senior citizens from below the chin to the floor.

I wonder if former President Harry S. Truman, the first U.S. citizen to sign up for Medicare in 1965 (with the-current prez Lyndon Johnson looking over his shoulder), knew that Medicare wouldn't have enough bite to provide dental care?

Look, lots of people have much worse problems than I do. I understand that.

I'm just saying that spending a ton of out-of-pocket money on having root canal prep (i.e. drilling for oil) and another tooth pulled on the same day in one dental session ain't no Fourth of July picnic with apple pie a la mode.

I can't even ease the financial pain with a chilled glass of Chardonnay. I'm on antibiotics, you see. I may have mentioned I'm having some dental issues.

You took the part that once was my heart

So why not why not take all of me

Sing it, Frank. Sing "All of Me" like you're singing it just for all of us on Medicare.

SHE COULDN'T MEDICARE LESS

My doctor broke up with me today.

She wants to see other people. Younger people. And she wants me to see other people as well.

She doesn't care who I see, just as long as it isn't her.

"Did you see the sign out front? As of January 1, I'm not treating Medicare patients anymore," she said, shortly before getting physical with me for the last time.

"The doctor won't see you now." How did I misread those signs?

On my last few visits, my doctor, whom I'm convinced is a caring soul but is also someone who's had it way past "up to here" with government red tape associated with Medicare patients, has complained about having to lug around her laptop computer to deal with patients like me. You know, those who have committed the mortal sin of letting the clock tick too many times to suit those younger.

I've been grandfathered in before, but this is the first time I've ever been grandfathered out.

In as gentle voice and nicest tone I could muster during my physical -- after all, she was reaching for the rubber gloves -- I said, "I can certainly understand your frustration, but it sort of leaves guys (and women) like me out in the cold. We have a doctor we really like and trust, and now we can't go to them anymore."

I don't remember exactly what my doctor said to that. I was too concerned about her opening up the examination room door and calling for the nurse. Any guy who's ever had his prostate checked knows what that means. (That reminds me, the car needs an oil change.)

I do remember that she didn't say, "Oh, excuse me. I forgot for a second that you are one of my original patients. You came with me to start this practice when I was struggling and you've been a loyal patient for years. And you have referred several people to me, who, by the way, are not on Medicare and pay retail. So, of course, I'll treat you and be here for you as long as you need me, even if I do have to use this laptop computer and deal with a little red tape and, yes, reduced revenue. Have you seen what I'm driving? I think I can stand the slight financial inconvenience to care for loyal, longtime patients like you."

Nope, she didn't say anything like that. I still can't believe I misread those earlier signs of approaching detachment. Since that rather abrupt, "See 'ya" visit, I have noticed some other signs, though. Like the physicians' Hippocratic Oath:

"I will remember that I do not treat a fever chart, a cancerous growth, but a sick human being, whose illness may affect the person's family and economic stability. My responsibility includes these related problems, if I am to care adequately for the sick."

A couple of my friends have mentioned something like, "It's nothing personal. It's just business."

Really? Does "care for a patient" merely mean reading medical charts and graphs, taking X-rays and prescribing pills? Just business refers to my banker, or the cashier at the grocery store who barely even looks up at customers these days.

I think not. Our personal care physician takes our blood, asks us what's going on and treats us, dammit, physically and sometimes a little mentally as well. "You've gained a little weight since your last visit. Is something bothering you? Is everything all right?"

And, excuse me, doctor, but I'd like to point out one more paragraph from the Hippocratic Oath, which, by the way, is not the Hypocritic oath:

"I will remember that there is art to medicine as well as science, and that warmth, sympathy, and understanding may outweigh the surgeon's knife or the chemist's drug."

It has never ceased to amaze me that even those a decade or so younger than people of Medicare age seem to have no notion that they, too, will soon be considered too old to be taken seriously in many areas or even given equal medical consideration.

It's coming, doctor, quicker than you realize. May you be treated more respectfully and with more caring consideration when your time comes.

Yes, my doctor broke up with me today. Sadly, she left me for a younger patient.

I'm not litigious, generally. But I am thinking about demanding illimony.

GEORGE 'WHAT-A-SHOW' JONES

You know, George Jones is coming back to the Opry for the last time.

Aw, we all wondered if he would.

You know, it keeps runnin' through my mind ...

This time, he's over his troubles for good.

George Jones, the conflicted superstar country music troubadour with a pure voice of the gods and a devil's grip on whiskey bottles, will play the Grand Ole Opry one more time.

According to an article published on The Hollywood Reporter website, a public funeral for Jones, who died Friday at 81, will be held Thursday (May 2, 2013) at 10 a.m. at Nashville's country music shrine.

"George would have wanted his fans and friends everywhere to be able to come and pay their respects along with his family," said publicist Kirt Webster in a press release quoted by The Hollywood Reporter.

As much as I'd like to be in Nashville to pay my respects, I can't. So two unforgettable meetings, regrettably from afar, with the greatest country music crooner of all time (in my humble opinion) will have to do.

I worked my way up to San Antonio from a small-but-proud newspaper (The Valley Morning Star) in Harlingen in 1983. It didn't take long to become aware that The San Antonio Stock Show & Rodeo was a big deal for my new city and for my new newspaper, The San Antonio Light.

The rodeo became a big deal for me as well when I learned that George Jones would be appearing the night our group from the newspaper planned to go. The rodeo itself was fun enough, though distinct with *odor-de-livestock*.

I moved to the edge of my seat, though, when Jones and his band was introduced. The country superstar came out and sang his opening number just fine. Jones was well into doing a great job on Tune No. 2 as well when some stupid jerk in the audience flung a cowboy hat like a Frisbee that somehow -- and I still don't understand quite how -- sailed far enough to hit Mr. Jones right in the kisser.

"Well, good night y'all," Jones said calmly. He turned around and left the stage after performing for a total of about four minutes and never looked back.

About a decade later, I had another chance at Jones, who was dubbed "No Show Jones" by many back then. The Possum and his band booked a gig at a festival at Austin's Town Lake (now Lady Bird Lake).

I was dating future wife Suellen then, and I couldn't wait to impress her with decent seats to see George Jones. Suellen's daughter Lisa, about 10 or 11 at the time, was with us. It was a great day. The festival, face-painting for Lisa and then, if he showed up, George Jones.

The good news is that Mr. Jones did show up, and he seemed to be (relatively) sober. Jones' entourage even sold T-shirts flaunting the obvious: "I saw No Show Jones."

George Jones took the stage with a friendly grin shortly after the sun went down over the lake that night. His voice, clear and full of nuance (and perhaps Jim Beam Kentucky bourbon), echoed through the speakers like vocal nectar.

Jones was in fine voice that night. And so was the drunk seated directly behind me who -- leaning forever forward spewing breath that reeked of the devil's outhouse -- matched Jones word for word, nuance for nuance ... only louder and directly into my ears!

We didn't even care. We were there and so was George Jones. What a memorable night.

Thanks for showing up, George. We'll miss you.

As George himself would say:

"Yabba dabba doo, the king is gone."

GONGED, BUT NOT FORGOTTEN

I had to chuckle when I was asked to help spread the word about an upcoming Gong Shorts Film Competition.

My uneasy, slightly painful deep-seated laughter had nothing to do with the actual event, where original short films (3-15 minutes long on DVD) are guaranteed a 3-minute play before audience members are allowed to call for the, uh, gong.

I have memories of another local, live gong show way back in the '70s, you see, where I -- quite by accident, I might add -- was ... uh ...

I was gonged by a chimpanzee. OK, there, I said it!

According to the first dictionary within reach, chimpanzees are defined as "a great ape with large ears, mainly black coloration, and lighter skin on the face, native to the forests of western and central Africa. Chimpanzees show advanced behavior such as the making and using of tools."

In this case, Deena the Chimp's tool of choice was a gong.

Picture this: a North Dallas nightspot that featured a live gong show where up-and-coming and/or down-and-going comedians gathered on Thursday nights to wow audiences with their wildly funny wit or get gonged and laughed out of the joint a la a cheap imitation of *The Gong Show* produced and hosted on TV in the afternoons by Chuck Barris in the mid and late-'70s.

The audience didn't get to vote at the Dallas gong show, though. A distinguished panel of judges, including, if memory serves correctly, the late, great Jerry Haynes, the WFAA-TV personality also known as Mr. Peppermint, the show's organizer and the aforementioned Deena the Chimp.

Deena, you see, was not your run-of-the-mill primate. Deena was billed by owner and Rent-A-Chimp proprietor Mike Stower as "the world's only stripping chimp."

Obviously, it was a very high class operation. I had stopped performing comedy for free about then, having heard, "We'd love for you to come out and entertain, but of course we can't pay you anything" too many times.

I was holding steadfast to my rule, too. But -- to give you some idea of how lean things were about then -- if I wanted to buy lunch, it was very likely that I'd need to sell some blood to do it.

I only agreed to perform at the gong show because of two things: There was a $50 cash prize, and the organizer assured me that I would win and could breeze in, do five minutes of snappy comic patter and be out of there in a flash 50 bucks richer.

Words I'll never forget (although I'll keep trying): "I've seen the other comedians. It's a sure thing. You will be the winner!"

If I learned anything that night, it was not to underestimate (or perhaps overestimate) a chimpanzee that strips for her bananas.

At about the 3-minute mark, I was rolling pretty good. I could see the audience responding well to my hilarious material. I also saw Mr. Peppermint having a good time. Then my eyes -- about to fill with utter fear -- spotted Deena with the gong mallet in her paw/hands. (Come on people, don't you know not to give a chimp the mallet at an EXPLETIVE DELETED, EXPLETIVE DELETED, EXPLETIVE DELETED gong show?)

If that wasn't bad enough, Deena must have had a cold. I saw her fighting back a sneeze just as the audience was really laughing at my Class A Prime material.

Let's cut to the sad chase: The sneeze exploded. Deena's mallet hand/paw jerked in the direction of the gong and BLAM! I began thinking about where I might be selling blood for lunch the next day.

Oh, and one more thing:

Why Deena, why?

LET'S ALL DRIVE TO THE SNACK BAR

It just occurred to me that when I was growing up in the 1950s and '60s in Grand Prairie, Texas, I was also growing up at drive-in movie theaters.

I bet many of you did too.

For me, it was mainly the Downs Drive-in on Main Street on the West side of town, at least in the earlier years of my youth. That's when I can still remember dangling my feet and stretching my foot way down to kick the dirt (and a few red ants) below the swing set on the playground in front of the screen.

Later, my drive-in experiences became increasingly less idyllic. In fact, they became downright scary at times as my child's eye morphed into pre-teen, teenage and adult-year vision. The trips to the swings gave way to eye-popping moments, like when my older brother let me tag along with him and his friends.

I was in the backseat as we ventured all the way to Chalk Hill (and the Chalk Hill Drive-in) when I was 13 or 14. My brother and his buddies were there to check out girls, so the movie choice didn't matter at all to them.

Their eyes wandered as my brother and his buds concentrated on female traffic walking by. I, on the other hand, was locked into a shell-shocked stare as "Elmer Gantry" (1960), the adult-themed tale of a fast-talking, boozing title character "evangelist" portrayed with fire and, perhaps, brimstone in his eyes by Burt Lancaster (in an Oscar-winning performance), seared the screen.

I miss drive-in movies. Although a few are hanging on in this high-tech new century, they represent a bygone era that kids and youngsters today will never get to experience.

So my question of the day: Is it possible to grow up properly without skinned knees from drive-in playgrounds, the smell of 10-

cent popcorn in the car and the experience of driving off while forgetting a speaker is attached to the car window?

I suppose so. But who would want to?

MIRACLE ON SOUTHEAST 11TH STREET

I was 10 in 1957, and all I wanted for Christmas that year was a record player. Not just any record player, but a state-of-the-art red with white top portable fold-up unit that could play 45s as well as albums and, yes, 78s.

You know that kid Ralphie in the movie "A Christmas Story" (1983) who really, really wanted a Red Ryder BB gun in the 1940s? Well, that was me in the '50s, except I thought life would not be worth living unless Santa, or Old Santa Claus as my Dad called him, delivered the record player.

I knew we didn't have much money back then, but I never considered us poor. Poor people didn't have much of anything to eat. I'm not saying we had meat every night, though. Supper in our modest little neighborhood on the southeast side of Grand Prairie (between Dallas and Fort Worth) often included a creative combination of leftovers Mother called hash. Or we dined on cornbread and red beans.

Dad, who always dreamed of busting out to bigger things (not unlike this scribe), walked rain or shine the three or four blocks to and from The Plant five days a week, carrying a jet black lunch box. Chance Vought Aircraft was the official name of the aircraft factory at the time. I never heard Dad call it anything other than The Plant. And for the short periods of time my brother Lannie and I worked there later, it was The Plant for us as well.

I wasn't worried about disrupting the family budget for something as extravagant as a $19.95 state-of-the-art red with white top portable fold-up record player that could play 45s as well as albums and, yes, 78s. After all, that one would be on Santa, not the meager Ratliff family budget.

At first I hinted. After all, I was clearly headed for some kind of career in show business. All I had at the time was the desire, and that desire for some kind of spotlight in the performing arts was definitely my destiny. (I proved that a few years later when I was awarded the privilege of announcing fried chicken specials over the loudspeaker while working as a checker at Safeway.)

As Christmas drew near, I panicked and spelled out succinctly and with gusto how necessary the red record player with the cool white top was to my future.

It was three days before Christmas in 1957 when my Mother and Dad pulled up in front of the A&P on Main Street with me in the backseat and issued specific instructions:

"We'll be back in a few minutes," Dad said. "You wait right here."

I saw my parents walk past A&P and duck into Skillern's drugstore next door. Like the good son I thought I was, I did wait in the car.

For a minute. Then I made a fatal mistake that still haunts me to this day, let's see, 57 years later.

I slithered out of our Chevy and hugged the A&P wall until I reached the plate glass at Skillern's. Sticking just enough of my face in front of the window to get a peek with one eye, I saw my Dad talking to a clerk. The $19.95 state-of-the-art red with white top portable fold-up record player that could play 45s as well as albums and, yes, 78s was on the counter between them and Dad was reaching for his wallet in his left pocket.

Elated, I was just about to turn and sneak back to the car when a chill shot up my spine that took decades to fade and still lingers deep down inside today. My Dad spotted me in the window and our eyes locked; a hurtful look of a trust broken in his, terror in mine.

Before my feet got the signal from my startled brain to get the heck out of there, time froze. I remember seeing my Dad shake his head "No thanks, I changed my mind" to the clerk as his hand eased his wallet back into its resting place.

When my parents got back in the car, nothing was said. I knew what that meant. And my folks knew that I knew. The rest of the usually festive days leading up to Christmas Day were a stunned blur. Mother made her wonderful fudge as usual; loaded with pecans for everyone except me with a little plate just for me with no nuts.

The fudge didn't seem quite as sweet that year. My life was over. How would I ever find my place in the spotlight without the red-and-white record player to foster my love for music, to hear Bill Haley & His Comets sing "Rock Around the Clock"? The only song running through my head on Christmas Eve that year was Buddy Holly and the Crickets singing "That'll Be the Day (When I Die)."

My brother beat me to the Christmas tree that year. I wasn't exactly feeling it, if you know what I mean. From behind him, though, I got a glimpse of something red and white. Then, all of a sudden, there it was, my very own $19.95 state-of-the-art red with white top portable fold-up record player that could play 45s as well as albums and, yes, 78s!

That's why I believe in Old Santa Claus. And forgiveness. And second chances. And that's why I always will.

OH NO, I JUST SAID YES

There's so much hurt, so much negativity in the world right now. This is one man's attempt to spin things in a more positive direction.

I decided to go one entire day without saying no to anyone.

"Just Say Yes" is what I call my revolutionary experiment to tilt world karma back to a more positive stance. Let's just say it turned out to be a day that will live in infamy for me, if not bankruptcy court or jail.

Or Utah.

Well, I'm a Mormon now. That's quite a departure for a guy who grew up Southern Baptist. But Ezekiel and Mitch launched my new religious enlightenment with a determined knock on the front door before my trusted roommate, Mr. Coffee, even began to drip.

As per my plan for new world harmony, I couldn't respond negatively to the two smiling disciples in black slacks and white shirts. I'm much too private a person to feel comfortable with door-to-door badgering, uh, soliciting, I mean enlightenment. But I suppose I'll get used to it.

I am very keen on the bicycle, though. With spring in full bloom, I can't wait to ride it around White Rock Lake on lazy, relaxing weekend days.

Oh, I guess Sundays are out.

Word must have spread pretty quickly about my "Just Say Yes" day. I've got two new credit cards and three and a half cases of Girl Scout cookies. That should earn little Mattie (or her mom) some kind of merit badge.

The second new credit card of the day was interesting. It promised a credit line of up to $2,500. Did you know those pie-in-the-sky credit card come-ons have a tiny asterisk beside the dollar figure?

When I called to activate the card, a very nice woman (Dorothy, I think) acted like I had just won the lottery.

"Mr. Ratliff (slight pause) I am pleased to inform you that based on your credit status we are able to extend to you a credit line of ... (dramatic pause) ... $450."

"What did you say," I muttered in disbelief, losing my positive attitude for the tiniest split second.

I couldn't refuse on this day, of course. But I have thought once or twice about the $59 annual membership fee, the $29 over-limit fee (which is sure to come into play) and the dreaded cash advance fee. No problem there. There's not enough room on my measly credit ceiling to get any cash.

I'm not one to dwell too long on negative things, especially not on this life-changing day. Besides, I was way too busy. I changed Internet providers a couple of times, took advantage (at the urging of a sweet-sounding, but resolute lady named Doris, I think) of my right to choose my electricity provider and switched my long distance service to MCI.

No, check that, I just got a call from AT&T.

"Can you hold on for a minute, AT&T (a very nice, if slightly determined young woman named Becky)? I've got Dillard's on the other line. Then, wow, I need to return a call to a TV satellite dish company." I missed that call while I was out getting fast food and, yes, super-sized for the first of two times during the day.

Question to self: Do we really need a 52-ounce drink to wash down a burger and Freedom Fries (lots and lots of Freedom Fries)?

I fought the urge to refuse to be super-sized at supper. But a deal's a deal. Besides, I was committed to complete the day of total abstinence from negativity.

I was pretty hungry anyway. You can't visit your two new lake lots and time-share condo (Enid, Oklahoma?) without working up a frisky appetite.

Looking back, though, I'd have to say the evening brought the most startling surprise. That's when I met my fiancée, Yi Ha.

Boy, wait till our future children hear the wacky way we met. I was driving along Northwest Highway, on my way home after giving blood, when I spotted her standing by the road. Well, sort of out in the road.

Actually, I suppose she saw me first. And talk about love at first sight. Before the light even turned green, my intended professed her devotion and loyalty – once I rolled down the window, of course.

I'll never forget the first words out of her mouth. Yi Ha looked me straight in the eye (On second thought, it could have been a little lower) and introduced herself.

"Yi Ha! I love you long time."

I'd give anything to report that becoming engaged, which I remember thinking should please the Mormons once we arrive in Utah, turned out to be the perfect nightcap to a very busy day of bringing positive energy into the troubled world.

Truth is, though, ever since I gave Yi Ha my pin numbers I haven't actually seen her.

What could I do? She asked. I couldn't say no.

Just before I barfed midway through my second box of Thin Mints, though, a surprisingly cheerful notion hit me.

She can't get far on 450 bucks minus the membership fee.

STRANGE BEDFELLOWS

Film critics don't get many death threats. On major daily newspapers (Remember those?), anger-driven threats are usually blurted out to political columnists or someone dumb enough to mess with the layout of the crossword puzzle or TV schedule.

I got an impassioned death threat in the wee hours of the morning of Oct. 4, 1985, though. It all began shortly after severely withered movie idol Rock Hudson, who had kept his homosexuality secret from his fans for decades, succumbed in Beverly Hills weighing a mere 140 pounds.

The next day, I was charged with writing the obituary for the Oscar-nominated star of "Giant," "Pillow Talk" and "The Undefeated" for the San Antonio Light newspaper.

"And don't forget to mention that he died of AIDS," my editor mentioned casually over his shoulder as he walked away.

That sounded a lot like a straight news story to me. Why me? Film critics prefer something other than the grit and grime of real life. That's why many of us became film critics in the first place. We like to sit in a dark room and be transported off to somewhere wonderful like Oz or Willy Wonka's chocolate factory or -- if that's not possible -- to the concession stand where Milk Duds await.

It only took me a few seconds to realize that the San Antonio Light was not my rodeo to run. So I wrote what seemed to me at the time to be a glorious bit of prose about Hudson's long career that began as a truck driver and hanging around outside the movie studio gates in Hollywood passing out glamor stills of himself. If we can believe Hollywood legend, and why the heck can't we?, a movie publicist coined the phrase "beefcake" with the square-jawed Rock Hudson (real name Roy Harold Scherer Jr.) in mind.

And, since the Associated Press had already spilled the beans, I included the fact that Hudson, widely beloved for his squeaky clean romps in the cinematic sack with Doris Day and other starlets, had succumbed to AIDS.

You must know this. AIDS is a horrible disease these days. In the early and mid-'80s, it was a mystery disease that killed people -- primarily gay men -- in a raging storm of controversy.

So the next day my Rock Hudson obit hit the streets. That night, or I should say about 3 the next morning, a telephone ring (probably about the 20th ring) rattled me out of my slumber.

"If you write that Rock Hudson died of AIDS again, I'm going to kill you," an almost shrieking person shouted into my ear.

This is the point in our little one-sided conversation here that I'd like to report that without missing a beat I quipped back, "I don't think Rock Hudson is going to die of anything again. Once pretty much does it, as far as we know."

I didn't, though. I froze, then checked to make sure the doors were all locked and went back to bed thinking, "Hey, somebody is actually reading this stuff."

The next day I casually mentioned to my colleagues at the paper that I -- a film critic, no less -- had gotten a death threat during the night. Let's just say the editors sprang into immediate action; insisting that I report the incident to the police right away. Their prompt concern impressed me until I finally realized that they were just protecting themselves in the event of my untimely demise and a possible lawsuit by my heirs.

The two police officers who showed up at my house -- you know, the scene of the crime -- appeared to be right out of Central Casting. We've all seen this scenario at the movies on a regular basis. There was literally one grizzled vet two weeks away from retirement and a rookie still getting used to all the free doughnuts.

"The caller said what, that he would kill you?" the rookie asked excitedly, jotting everything down furiously in his notepad. "Yes he did," I replied, catching a discreet glimpse of the beat-weary cop staring idly out the window into my backyard.

The last time I saw a grin that big on a policeman was years later when I was pulled over for doing 80 in a 55 trying to get down to the Blue Bell Ice Cream factory in Brenham for a Fourth of July celebration.

THE REAL COLD WAR

D espite what you may have heard on the news, the Cold War isn't over.

It rages on with me, a slightly bloated army of one. I'm deeply entrenched and flailing away on the front lines of a fierce, ongoing, losing battle.

I have this little ice cream issue, you see.

I wouldn't really call it an addiction, as such. To me, it's more like the cold, creamy, slippery slope to self-esteem hell.

It started out innocently enough. I remember sneaking into the kitchen in the middle of the night as a kid of 10 or 11 in Grand Prairie, Texas. While my family slept, I'd stand in the harsh glare of the refrigerator light and my nagging conscience. Degrading myself with one teaspoon of frozen self-esteem poison at a time.

It was the cheap stuff back then; three-for-a-dollar iced milk. It tasted like frozen Elmer's Glue-All with a hint of cheap chocolate.

It made no difference to me. I'd scoop away, out of control (and often shivering), until one tiny teaspoon remained. Then I'd carefully replace the carton in the freezer and shamefully hope no one noticed that some thief in the night had gone on a binge.

For many years, my dad (who died in 2001) loved to tell the story about the time he replaced a flimsy carton I had previously ravaged with a brand-new one. Same generic brand. Same dull flavor. For once, my mom, dad and older brother got to enjoy an ice cream-like concoction at their leisure while I waited for my next target.

Good one, Dad.

In adulthood, the situation has gotten worse, not better. Needless to say, if my addiction were to a more lethal drug - say cocaine or "Lara Croft" video games - my life would be over. I'd be sleeping in a cardboard box outside some Baskin-Robbins store.

Don't get me wrong. I fight it. And I lose. Last winter, for instance, I had gone two or three weeks without giving in. But on the coldest, most miserable night of the year, I caved. It was sleeting. Every step outside was a precursor of doom and perhaps a visit to ER (not the TV show).

"If you don't absolutely have to go out, stay home," the weather guy in the loud bow tie was saying.

I absolutely had to go out.

I bundled up and gingerly made my way to the car, which was shrouded in a thick sheet of ice. De-icing would take at least 10 or 15 minutes. So I drove the four blocks to my neighborhood 7-Eleven at about 5 mph with my head sticking out the window like a flop-eared dog -- a flop-eared dog with icicles.

That's nothing, though, compared to the time a few years ago when I inadvertently swallowed a knife during a binge.

I don't exactly have patience when my craving gets the best of me. I have this dangerous -- ludicrous, in fact -- habit of chiseling chunks of rock-hard ice cream from the carton with a dinner knife.

One night, in my haste, I plunged into a solidly frozen half gallon of Rocky Road with a knife and reckless abandon. I plopped the chunk of instant gratification into my mouth. And I pulled back a rather incomplete table utensil.

A piece of the knife - about the size of a thumbnail - was missing. Since this kind of gluttony knows no shame and obviously makes no sense, I rushed through the rest of the abusive ritual.

The thinking, if we can call it that:

"I'd better hurry. This just might be my last shot at Rocky Road."

I'm happy to report that no dire consequences resulted. Once the empty euphoria of gorging had passed and was replaced by guilt, I thought that, at the very least, I'd have a difficult time getting through the metal detector at the airport.

I think the knife tip is still lodged somewhere in my body. I think it's in my "yet." I don't know which internal organ a "yet" is exactly. But I'll never forget a television news anchor reporting one night about a poor woman who had been shot.

"She survived," the golden-throated anchor said, "but the bullet remains in her yet."

Hopefully, the unwelcome foreign object won't relocate to a more easily damaged organ for either of us.

With a little luck and about $10,000 worth of therapy, I might just get this Chunky Monkey off my back before it's too late. I may not be so fortunate the next time a concealed sharp steel object rides the Blue Bell Express into my Homemade Vanilla-coated internal abyss.

TRUE CONFESSION:
THE COLD FACTS

I've been sneaking around, and I'm terrified my wife is going to find out.

Yet how can I resist her warm embrace?

Surely, someone out there will understand, even if it's only the men; some perhaps suffering the same agony.

She's there to warm me and protect me from the cold abyss of the outside world. She's always there when I need her, and she never utters even a hint of objection or complaint.

She is ... my thermostat.

I'm cold natured. I can't help it. I can't deny it. I can't defend it. So I sneak around to deal with it, but the deceit gnaws away at my soul. Not enough, though, to shiver all day when I'm home alone during cold winter months.

My wife Suellen, through no fault of her own, has an inner body temperature that appears to reside in the desert of El Azizia, Libya, which is generally regarded as the hottest place on Earth. How does 136 degrees sound?

So, especially during the winter months, if Suellen is anywhere near comfortable, I feel like I'm trudging naked through a raging blizzard in Antarctica.

I've tried to fight the good fight; wrap myself in blankets, wear socks in house shoes, etc. But occasionally I have to poke my nose out of my blanket pile to move around. And there it is. I'm right back in the frozen tundra.

"This is why humans moved into caves, then built huts and eventually took out second mortgages on houses in the suburbs," I plead, "to get out of harsh elements like this."

That argument never flies, of course.

"If you're cold, just put some more clothes on," she says.

To which I've been known to reply:

"If you're hot, you could just take some clothes off."

Gentlemen, I don't recommend that retort.

If you just blurt it out anyway, as I have, just say something like...

"What? I didn't say anything. I was shivering so much you just heard my teeth clicking together."

And so it goes, season after season. That's why I've resorted to my savior of warmth, Ms. Thermostat.

We heat it up toasty style during winter days. I just have to remember to restore the chill before Suellen comes home.

The deceit is killing me, though.

I can't go on living this lie. So I'm fessing up and embracing the mantra of that great philosopher Vanilla Ice.

If there was a problem yo I'll solve it

Check out the hook while my DJ revolves it

Ice ice baby, indeed.

HOW'S THE NEW YEAR'S RESOLUTION GOING?

S orry, I just had to ask, primarily because mine is going so well.

Not that I want to gloat, but I've lost enough weight that our bathroom scale is now down into the numbers range. It wasn't always that way.

For longer than I care to remember, that little window on the scale -- the dreaded eye into our soul of self-loathing, if you will -- didn't show any numbers at all, just letters or words.

"One at a time" was probably my favorite at the highest point of actual weight and lowest ebb of self-esteem.

Then, after some half-tries to do something about my situation, I eased down into the "OMG!" range and, finally, after self-discipline which I figure equals the resolve of "The Little Engine That Could," I got the scale to merely whimper "Help" for a while.

Now I'm down into numbers, baby, and descending with the not-so-blazing speed of a packed elevator at the end of a long day touring the refried bean factory.

I guess you're wondering how I pulled off this amazing success. Easy ...

We got bikes!

We bought them at night, in a hurry. What could possibly go wrong?

Plenty, actually. My wife Suellen's fun-on-two-wheels machine actually turned out to be a semi-rusted demonstrator suffering from *MacArthur Park* syndrome. You know, the song? Except it wasn't the cake left out in the rain. In this case, it was her bicycle, which will actually reluctantly shift a gear or two after five or six squirts of WD-40 and some serious handlebar-grip twisting.

My shiny new ride is a Huffy. I like to refer to it as a Huffy Puffy, mainly because we have some gently sloping hills in our neighborhood that appear to transform into Pikes Peak with speed bumps once I'm on the saddle.

(Saddle: The proper name for a bicycle seat, which I think was invented by a disturbed man or woman who enjoyed watching others suffer. Also, "bicycle seat sore" just doesn't have a ring to it like "saddle sore" does.)

The hills in our 'hood may not actually jut 14,115 feet into the sky like that Pikes Peak thing, but it sure feels that way when I'm pedaling at about a thousand RPMs and tipping the speedometer at somewhere between 3/4 and 1 mph.

Not that I have a speedometer on my bike. I just know I'm not setting any speed records because a newborn puppy-dog just learning to stand on all fours beat me up the hill the other day. Also, it's common for people on that street to come out in their front yards to snicker at me (and, I suspect, place bets) as I sweat and pedal my way up the gradual slope.

Whatever. My diet and exercise program is working, so what do I care about how the neighbors feel? And just for the record, I'm pretty sure that little doggie is part greyhound. In fact, I'm declaring success. My New Year's resolution of 1979 has finally been accomplished. So congrats to me.

Now I can get serious about the next year's resolution: Become a world famous standup comedian before 1980 comes to an end.

I can't worry about that right now, though. Gotta go. It's time for my snack.

Yum, *frijoles refritos*.

DAD'S LATE-LIFE CRISIS

My dad moved out of the house one time, just couldn't take it anymore.

It's true, I suppose, that such a sudden chaotic shift in the family dynamic upsets children the most. My older brother and I were absolutely devastated.

After all, we were only in our early 40s.

"We're too old to come from a broken home," my brother quipped – or inwardly wept and tried to conceal it with a lame joke – as he broke the news to me on the phone.

"Daddy moved out. He took a room down by the golf course."

Two rapid-fire thoughts pin-balled through my brain with the speed and force of a 7-Eleven Slurpee headed for numbing brain-freeze on a hot August afternoon.

First, the fact that the words "moved out" and "golf course" occupied the same sentence spelled an approaching forbidding doom that had been mounting between my parents for some time; since his retirement from a factory job he probably hated for years, but endured to support the family.

Secondly, and for some odd reason slightly more disturbing to me, why did two grown men still refer to their father as Daddy and their mom Mother?

I couldn't worry about the name thing much at the time. There were more pressing matters. But here's a clue, I suppose. We named our dog Tip. Please don't laugh. (Oh go ahead.)

Quickly, my brother and I set about to "make things right again." A bolt of lightning had split our family tree into two broken half-trunks. Neither was complete, in our eyes, without its "better half."

Bitter half is a much better term. There had been tension between our parents for at least two decades. At heart, our dad was an entrepreneur, a gambler of sorts. Earlier in his life there was no need to add the "of sorts" on the end of gambler.

In his youth, our dad had traveled almost the entire United States leading teams of door-to-door magazine salesmen. From his native Hico in Central Texas, Daddy worked his way to New York City in one direction, then all the way down to California.

While his magazine sales teams were working the suburban neighborhoods of mid-to-late 1930s and early 1940s America, our dad would earn a little – and sometimes a lot – of extra cash in pool halls; the dens of iniquity chastised so thoroughly in "The Music Man."

"Trouble. That rhymes with P and starts with T. I'm talking TROUBLE, my friends."

Mother hated pool halls. And when Daddy found solace substituting golf in his later retirement years, she grew to despise that as well.

It probably wasn't just the fringe, early stages of her losing battle with Alzheimer's disease. As long as I can remember, Mother kept to herself. Her own mom abandoned my mother and her siblings when she was just a child. No doubt that nudged her in the general direction of being, especially in her later years, a recluse.

She loved two things with a passion: coffee and cigarettes. (Three things counting her boys.) Earlier, when I was in my mental and physical formative years, she also loved movies. Some of my happiest memories involve staying up late to watch the late, late movie with Mother.

Before that, when Daddy and Mother were dating, they both loved movies and, presumably, each other. They used to gather up their dimes and indulge in triple features. I know they did. They both shared that with me at different times.

Rotten memories tend to dominate the brain when a relationship begins to sour, though. My brother and I were long gone when the emotional crisis reached the breaking point.

We don't know exactly what happened, only that one Thanksgiving the parental visit required two stops. Mother pretended nothing was wrong; kept it all in like she always did. She welcomed us "home" as usual, but seemed to be clutching her coffee cup a little tighter than usual, inhaling the Salem Light a little deeper.

A few blocks away we found Daddy sitting in his old creaky recliner with the familiar table lamp on his right. A large jar of Planter's Peanuts were in the spotlight, just like they always were. But this wasn't home. It was if a vengeful tornado had simply lifted him up out of his house and plopped him down in a back, spare bedroom he was renting from a friend.

LINDSAY LOHAN'S SLAMMER JAM: NO TWEETING

Oh the inhumanity!

According to a People magazine article by Ken Lee, newly arrived Lynwood, CA jail resident Lindsay Lohan can't Tweet or smoke while she's serving a 90-day parole violation jail sentence that'll likely result in only a couple weeks of slammer time.

And, if the "Mean Girls" co-star was wearing hair extensions on the way in, they have been, shall we say, unextended. The extensions, if there were any, would be returned to Lohan on the way out.

"According to a jail insider, Lohan will be housed in a 12-by-8 cell next to E! reality TV star Alexis Neiers, 19, who's currently at Lynwood on a six-month sentence for her part in burglarizing Orlando Bloom's house.

"But Neiers got the more famous digs: She's in the cell once occupied by Paris Hilton," the People magazine article adds.

Maybe Lohan can't Tweet, but that doesn't mean she can't communicate with the outside world. Twitter dispatches can be passed along to others to post for her during visitations.

And here's another major blow to the "dignity" of the formerly good actress ("Mean Girls," "A Prairie Home Companion") who has evolved for whatever reason (I have my theories) into a glam "bad girl" celebrity. Name-brand products are banned behind bars.

For a semi-starlet who feeds on the ever-present glare of the paparazzi spotlight, that's the equivalent of being forced to seek out generic products on Rodeo Drive in Beverly Hills.

Jokes are flying, of course. David Letterman said the other night that Lohan is already in trouble in jail for converting a shiv into a nail file. I got a hearty laugh Wednesday afternoon during a speaking engagement at Richland College in Dallas.

After being introduced, I thanked the audience for coming out in the sizzling, near 100 degree afternoon heat "for the Free Lindsay Lohan from Prison Rally."

Jail time is no laughing matter. So shame on all of us. And how dare authorities lock up a "celebrity" like Lohan and deprive her of her smokes, her Tweets and her hair extensions. (I'm not saying she was wearing any, but just in case she was.)

It could be worse, of course. Virgil Starkwell, the bumbling petty criminal played by Woody Allen in "Take the Money and Run," was thrown into a dusty, solitary confinement hole for a botched escape attempt. (He carved a gun out of soap./It rained on Escape Night./It happens.)

Prison guards put an annoying life insurance salesman in with Starkwell as the ultimate humiliation.

As far as I know, though, Virgil could have kept his hair extensions, if he was wearing any.

ONCE A KING WAS ENOUGH FOR ME

This is about the time I squared off for about a 20th of a round with boxing promoter Don King in the Las Vegas airport.

At a frozen yogurt stand at the Las Vegas airport, to be more exact.

Eight or 10 years ago I was returning from Los Angeles movie star interviews and had a 40 or 50-minute stopover between flights at the Sin City airport.

It only took me five minutes or so to lose $37 in the conveniently located airport slot machines. That was all I had on me, except for a fiver I kept for emergencies. So I looked around for another vice to keep me occupied until my flight was called.

"There it is," I said to myself as I wandered away from the ding-ding-ding of the alluring slots. "Frozen yogurt!"

You know frozen yogurt. It's that mystery chilled concoction, neither ice cream nor yogurt, really, that ice cream-a-holics like me shovel down with slightly less guilt than the full-fledged stuff that comes from the overly contented cows seen in TV commercials slurping down grass outside the Blue Bell ice cream factory in Brenham, Texas.

I was looking over the wall menu when I heard some commotion behind me. I looked around just in time to see Don King and his entourage nudging people in line aside as they plowed their way in unison -- like a well-trained NFL offensive line; No, more like a snowplow disrupting a tranquil neighborhood street full of playful kids -- to get to the counter.

"I don't care if it is Don King. They'll have to get through me if they want the No. 1 spot in line," I thought as my lips tightened and I prepared for battle.

Well, they got through me without much of a fuss (for them, at least). I floated out of their path with the slightest wimpy resistance. Unlike Muhammad Ali, I never quite got around to stinging like a bee.

I was seething and hot under the collar, though. In fact, I had to order a large to cool down after King and his court were gone.

I say all that to say this. Somewhere, Don King is celebrating his 81st birthday today. So, happy birthday, Mr. King. I hope you're enjoying a celebratory frozen yogurt without having to bluster your way to the front of some line today.

And I apologize for thinking what I wanted you to do with that frozen yogurt (cone and all) back in Vegas. I've calmed down since then.

Besides, I'm pretty sure that's not even humanly possible.

SHIRLEY, YOU CAN BE SERIOUS

I knew I was in big trouble when Shirley MacLaine walked into the room for our interview back in the mid '90s and was unhappy with the way the lights were set up.

At least I thought I knew. I was correct in assuming that meant a delay while the crew moved lights around (basically off me, on her) to Ms. MacLaine's satisfaction.

But that's all water under the bridge, or shadows under the bridge of my nose, as it were. After all, as the unsinkable movie star of five or six decades proclaims at the top of her website, "Life is a bowl of cherries ... Never mind the pits."

Today (April 24, 2012) is MacLaine's 78th birthday, so a couple of thoughts before moving on:

Happy birthday Shirley, Aurora Greenway ("Terms of Endearment" and "The Evening Star"), Ouiser Boudreaux ("Steel Magnolias"), Eve Rand ("Being There"), Charity ("Sweet Charity"), Irma La Douce ("Irma La Douce"), Fran Kubelik ("The Apartment"), Simone Pistache ("Can-Can"), Jennifer Rogers ("The Trouble with Harry") and all MacLaine's incarnations that came before.

Secondly, one my most anticipated movies in some time is Texas director Richard Linklater's "Bernie," which stars Jack Black and MacLaine and co-stars Texan Matthew McConaughey.

Based on actual macabre events that unfolded in the East Texas town of Carthage in the 1990s, "Bernie" revolves around the local mortician (Black) who befriended, then shot, then stuffed the wealthy "meanest" woman (MacLaine) in town into a freezer.

I'm pretty sure I sat down with MacLaine to chat about "The Evening Star" when we tripped the lights not so fantastic in 1996. To be honest, I traveled so much doing celebrity interviews back then all the luxury hotels, movie stars and room service tends to blur a little.

Let's just say "Total Recall" has long been merely a movie title for me.

That day in New York, Chicago or Los Angeles in some posh hotel suite temporarily disfigured by cables, cameras, lights and people (the crew, a diva's handlers) and an interviewer fighting flop sweat remains a vivid memory, however.

I was semi-terrified; nope, all the way there. As I sat almost knee-to-knee with a major movie star some might consider "difficult" while the crew tinkered with the lights, all I could think of was, "Say something, idiot!"

Before I could put my inept ignorance on full display, MacLaine (the purest definition of "seasoned pro"), took the lead and launched into comfortable, friendly chat to fill the time. In a complete about-face from the major star-interviewer dynamic, Ms. MacLaine took the opportunity to learn about me.

I've recalled that event many times (OK, not totally recalled). I appreciate the six-time Academy Award nominee and best actress winner for "Terms of Endearment" (1983) for being so gracious when she didn't have to be.

Maybe I reminded her of someone from her past. In another life perhaps; or -- Dare I think it? -- even a future one.

HENRY KISSINGER,
WHERE ART THOU?

I suppose at the age of 90, Henry Kissinger, Secretary of State for both Richard Nixon and Gerald Ford and the Nobel Peace Prize winner who negotiated a settlement of the Vietnam War, is probably not available to whip this country's international affairs in shape.

That's a shame because you'll never guess who it's come down to: An aging actor (of sorts) and a pierced, tattooed. over-the-hill athlete.

Dennis Rodman was in North Korea in February (2013), where he was apparently applauding the fact that Supreme Leader Kim Jong Un "once caught a fish this big."

You've probably heard about Rodman's trip to North Korea. He posed with Kim Jong Un, North Korea's Supreme Leader and Chief Rocket Launcher. They took in a basketball game or two, posed with the masses and sipped bubbly at dinnertime.

Rodman returned to the U.S., saying something like he'd worked out all the tension between this country and North Korea. The words had barely passed Rodman's pierced lips when North Korea's youngun -- sorry, Jong Un -- aimed his rockets at the U.S. and Austin specifically. I'm thinking the new supreme leader failed to get an invitation to Austin's South By Southwest Film Festival, which can be a tough ticket to snag. (This has yet to be confirmed, but I'm pretty darn sure that's what happened.)

Now, there's even bigger trouble looming on the volatile international scene.

Russia, it seems, has decided that fading Hollywood action star Steven Seagal, who once hinted to me that he was working or had worked in U.S. intelligence ("I can't talk about it. It's that secret," he said over lunch at the time.), is the perfect guy to be the -- And I am not making this up -- "face of a new campaign to promote Russian weapons."

That's right. According to published reports, "The 61-year-old American appears to be the unlikely choice to boost the country's arms sales as it makes a push to be the world's No. 1 exporter.

"Seagal accompanied Deputy Prime Minister Dmitry Rogozin to the Degtyarev gun manufacturing plant in Kovrov earlier.

"According to Russian news agencies, Mr. Rogozin said the actor may head up an international marketing campaign for the factory.

"He said: 'You're ready to fight American (manufacturers) with your teeth and your intellect, and if Americans are prepared to promote and support you, that says we're learning new ways to work on corporate warfare markets,'" a Sky.com article states.

One of my favorite phrases is, "Well, the world has still not gotten crazy enough for me."

I admit, though, with this news it's edging plenty close.

Oh brother, Henry Kissinger, where art thou?

MUST-SEE TV:
BALANCING THE UGLY

Excellence. TV news.

We don't see those words connected in thought much these days; not in a TV-watching era when local news anchors announce twice without any sort of correction that a man was arrested for "indacent" exposure instead of indecent exposure.

First the bad news, but stay with me. I promise some very good news is forthcoming. We are constantly barraged with a plethora of indecent exposure on TV these days from "Dancing with the Has-Been Stars" (Tommy Chong: Really, man?) to "Dating Naked" and too many so-so sitcoms to even count.

Check out the TV evening network news and you'll be inundated with a constant backwash of gruesome stories about ISIS militants beheading innocents, college students disappearing off college campuses and other carnage almost too grisly to mention; most recently a man in Florida calmly calling 911 to report to police that he had just shot and killed his daughter and his six grandchildren.

Now the good news. Let's make it the wonderful news. There's an oasis to be found in the TV airwaves that seem so glutted with depressing news sludge. It shines like a beacon of goodness, of hope and of people doing things not to bring the human race to the brink of a worm hole of depression and hate that we -- tired of endless worldwide despair -- appear to be all-too eager to leap into.

For lack of a better term, let's call it an offsetting balance to the ugly.

If you've never seen "CBS Sunday Morning," hosted by veteran CBS newsman Charles Osgood and airing at 8 a.m. in many markets; 7 in others and 9 in a few, I assure you that you are in for a treat.

Now I would like to issue a challenge to you -- yes you. I would like you to raise your right hand and say these words out loud:

"I, _____ _____, promise to watch one complete episode of "CBS Sunday Morning" before declaring to everyone I know that Larry Ratliff has finally lost it."

That's all I'm asking, just one full show without fast-forwarding, multitasking or in any other way (including snacking) distracting yourself from what I feel is the most intelligent television available today.

Granted, Osgood, whom CBS calls its poet-in-residence, is 81 now and is prone to leaning a bit to one side from time to time. What this remarkable journalist broadcaster brings, though, is smooth, confident calmness to a world many believe may be spinning out of control around him.

It all begins with the soothing notes of "Abblasen," a trumpet fanfare originally played in recording by Don Smithers, later Doc Severinsen, Johnny Carson's "Tonight Show" bandleader, and now by Wynton Marsalis.

Then there's Osgood, with a bow tie perhaps a little askew, standing beside an image of a welcoming sun, as if the world has another chance -- a new beginning -- to get things right.

And this show does get it right, offering a varied progression of extremely well-produced human interest, in-depth features and historical stories that might just make you wonder -- as it does my wife and me -- if the next segment can possibly measure up. But they do, and not solely because of Osgood, who is tremendous.

This is a show with an award-winning, experienced staff of behind-the-scenes people and reporters who know how to ask questions and report the news, whether it be a story about the Queen Mary, the infamous ocean liner that hasn't sailed in 50 years but is pretty much ready to go, to the finest Joan Rivers memoriam I saw.

My favorite reporter on the show is Martha Teichner, a former war correspondent and eight-time Emmy Award winner who joined CBS in 1977 and has worked on "CBS Sunday Morning" since 1993. If you'd like an example of Teichner's outstanding reporting, seek out one of her recent stories, "Monument Valley: Mother Nature's Scene-Stealing Movie Star," on the Internet.

And don't you dare think of "CBS Sunday Morning" as old-fogey news. There are stories of 11-year-olds making a difference in this world, for instance, and some younger journalists on the staff. I prefer not to judge the elders on the show by notches on the calendar, but as seasoned vets; able, smart, vibrant reporters and anchors wise beyond even their somewhat advanced years.

You learn things from watching this show, things that you will enjoy learning and that will enrich your life. Did you know, for instance, that the Queen Mary was so fast for its day that during World War II it outran German subs and even German torpedoes? You would know if you watched that episode.

My final point: The world is not really divided between the young and those older separated by a great abyss of misunderstanding. Sometimes the two can meet in a truly magical way. You might be amazed what really good journalists can do with the simple news that Tony Bennett and Lady Gaga recorded an album together.

Now repeat after me: "I, _____ _____, promise to watch one complete episode of "CBS Sunday Morning."

OH BOY, WHAT MOVIE
SHOULD I RENT?

I've often thought I missed my real chance to get wealthy as a film critic.

If I were in it for the money alone, I wouldn't have wasted my time writing about which movies to go see or rent, I'd just hang out in front of a popular video store and offer my expertise for cash on the spot.

A film critic as street performer, if you will. Crowdfunding, I believe, is the term being texted around these days.

The process would go something like this: You, confused by what movie to rent, would get out of your car in the parking lot of Blockbuster or other video store (when those were still around) and slouch toward the door.

Nine times out of 10 you knew you'd be overwhelmed by hundreds, perhaps thousands of choices inside. And, most of the time, you had already forgotten what title your spouse, significant other or child told you to get.

And then, there I'd be, right by the door with suggestions for latest arrivals, a really good foreign film, a classic or even, dare I mention it, a documentary. You would give me a dollar and move inside to rent your movie with confidence.

Oh, and I would get rich (counting on hordes of happy return customers, of course).

I said all that to say this. If I were standing in front of your favorite video store today, I would urge you to rent the superb documentary titled "Young @ Heart" that graced movie screens in 2007.

"Young @ Heart" chronicles the final weeks of rehearsal as the Young at Heart Chorus of Northampton, Mass. prepares for its annual concert series. This is not your usual chorus. For one thing, the average age is 81, and many of the chorus members have major health problems to overcome. Oh, and did I mention these vibrant seniors sing everything from James Brown to Sonic Youth.

The scene where they melt the hearts of young prisoners with their version of "Young @ Heart" will fill your heart with joy. "Young @ Heart" never gets better, though, than when the late Fred Knittle, a former World War II machine-gunner, sings a haunting version of Coldplay's "Fix You."

Knittle died at the age of 83 in 2009. He is survived by his wife, four children, 12 grandchildren, thousands of movie fans and one film critic you may know who desperately wanted to attend his funeral, but couldn't due to circumstances beyond his control.

IT'S A JUNGLE IN THERE
AND IN HERE

I had the pleasure of shaking Lassie's paw one time.

And I spent one very nervous, sleepless night in a five-star Beverly Hills hotel in 1997 directly across the hall from the snake about the size of a Buick that played the title role in the schlock-horror flick "Anaconda."

If I had to pick just one favorite movie animal, however, it wouldn't be a live one at all. I'm drawn to Dumbo, the baby elephant with enormous floppy ears drawn brilliantly by Disney animators "back in the day."

Oddly enough, the classic tale of a ridiculed circus elephant that achieves its full potential by making the most of those big ears when it counts was released on Halloween in 1941.

I don't know how old I was when "Dumbo" first flapped its ears and its movie magic on me, but it remains one of my fondest movie memories. It's also my first recollection of sharing a movie with my mom, who loved movies way back then as much as I do now.

If I might slither back to thoughts of that big ol' snake "Anaconda" for a minute, you may be wondering a couple of things: (1) What's a snake measuring roughly 20-feet-long doing in a five-star Beverly Hills hotel suite? and (2) How did I end up directly across the hall from it?

Let's begin with No. 2, since that's the one that troubled, puzzled and panicked me the most at the time. That's an easy question. The answer is "buzzard luck," which basically means that if anything bad is going to happen, it generally happens to your faithful scribe here.

And secondly, to question No. 1: The movie studios, which invite film critics from across the U.S. and Canada and most of the free world to fly to various locales to see an upcoming movie and interview the stars, occasionally go the extra publicity mile to make those interview opportunities into what they perceive to be "an event."

So some suit in a movie studio carpeted corner office decided it would be a dandy idea to show off an anaconda to the film press during the interview days. Forty or 50 film critics, entertainment writers and -- I can only hope -- giant snake wranglers showed up for the event.

"The movie studio wants us to remind you to please stop by Suite 1212 to see the snake used in 'Anaconda,'" the polished check-in person chirped. "Welcome back to the Four Seasons, Mr. Ratliff. Here's your key. You're in Suite 1213."

Are you beginning to understand how this "buzzard luck" curse works?

The door to Suite (and sour) 1212 was partially open when I nervously unlocked my door across the hall and threw down my luggage on the bed. I remember the spot because it's also where I almost threw up about five minutes later.

Being a good movie junket soldier, I crossed the hall and stepped lightly into Suite 1212. A movie studio rep welcomed me in, and two or three other movie critics were staring into the giant glass case that barely contained the anaconda.

I am not making this up: That snake, no, that giant snake locked its eyes on me and never altered its gaze. Even as other people milled about, the slithery creature -- and maybe I should be flattered by this -- only had eyes for me, tilting and moving its head this way and that as I tried to break the fixation.

I made a quick exit and double-locked my door until it was time to go to see the movie itself.

Upon my return to the 12th floor about 10 p.m., there were no movie studio reps in sight and no one milling about. (Had they all been eaten like unfortunate Jon Voight in the movie?)

As I clumsily fumbled for the credit card key to my room, I looked over my shoulder. The snake's door was still propped open. Light filtered out into the hall as if it was partially shielded by giant trees in the forest. Before I bolted into my room, I had to see for myself that the snake was still contained in that glass case. So I tip-toed ever so carefully to the open door and peeked in ...

THE SNAKE WAS STARING RIGHT INTO MY EYES AGAIN, as if it was just waiting for my return.

That was the only time I ever felt like a room service meal.

READY FOR BUDDY HOLLY LIVE-ISH?

I'm all for free enterprise, even when it comes to making a few bucks off dearly departed spouses to pay the rent and have a little left over for other essentials such as facelifts, body lowerings, tummy tucks, plastic breasts and, of course, lip-and-hip enhancement.

Heck, I hope when I'm gone my wife Suellen writes the book I've never had the guts to write (so far) about the bizarre path of a film critic trying to maintain his journalistic dignity while tip-toeing through the vague and veiled world of celebrity entertainment.

That said, I'm having more than a little trouble understanding why Maria Elena Holly, the Texas music icon's widow, has signed off on a virtual Buddy Holly stage tour set to kick off next year, according to a story in the Hollywood Reporter.

That's right, a hologram of Holly will likely sing -- sort of -- all the hits from "Peggy Sue" to "That'll Be the Day." Who knows? In this age of social media and anything-goes-don't bother-to-check-your-sources reporting, a flickering image of Holly might just sell a ton of tickets.

According to the Hollywood Reporter article:

"Hologram USA is already working on the hologram-like performance of the rock and roll icon, as well as on a similar show around Liberace, which will debut in Las Vegas. Through the partnership with Buddy Holly Licensing, the company has access to music and images of Holly. Interactive elements involving the audience and backup band members are also being created."

Surely, Holly's widow is fighting this sort of tales-from-the-crypt nonsense to sell tickets. That's what you and I and any sane person who respects what the guy in glasses from West Texas accomplished in such a short time in the spotlight would think. Right?

We would be wrong about that.

"I am so excited that my partnership with Hologram USA on the Buddy Holly concert project will allow a new generation of fans to experience the thrill of seeing Buddy 'live' and in concert for the first time in many decades," Maria Elena Holly told the Hollywood Reporter.

So sorry, Mrs. Holly, but no one is going to see your late, great -- let's just go ahead and say legendary -- husband again live or even, as you put it, 'live.'

The music genius from Lubbock died along with The Big Bopper and Ritchie Valens in a tragic plane crash between Clear Lake, Iowa and Moorhead, Minn. almost exactly 56 years ago. Holly was only 22 years old.

In "American Pie," Don McLean's meandering 1971 folk-rock anthem with almost hypnotic lyrics, McLean referred to Feb. 3, 1959 as "the day the music died."

I suggest we celebrate Holly best by just listening to his almost unbelievable collection of hits. And if you simply must see a semi-image of the man, seek out "The Buddy Holly Story," the 1978 biopic starring Gary Busey.

Yes, that Gary Busey; the human hologram who's pushing the Amazon Fire TV Stick in commercials and can't tell the difference between a Fire Stick and a seashell. Busey was on fire as Holly, by the way.

I know an Elvis Presley hologram concert is in the works as well. So why not go all the way? Bring back The Possum, the late, great George Jones, who died in April 2013. He could sing his signature hit, although it would have to be adjusted time wise.

You know, "He Stopped Loving Her Almost Two Years Ago Today."

But Buddy Holly in a hologram concert? Line up and enjoy yourself if you must. A word of advice: Don't bother waiting around for an autograph.

As for me, that'll be the day-ay-ay when I ... when I ... don't know.

I've got nothing. *Rave On*, indeed.

CLASSIC MOVIE LINES: A RETORT CARD

W e've all heard the infamous classic movie lines a hundred, perhaps a thousand times:

"Frankly, my dear, I don't give a damn." -- Clark Gable's Rhett Butler to Vivien Leigh's Scarlett O'Hara in "Gone With the Wind" (1939).

What we haven't heard, though, is a snappy comeback to those familiar lines entrenched in our subconscious.

Not until now, that is.

I've decided it's my civic duty, and perhaps my new life's work, to provide a comeback, a chance for the verbally one-upped to rattle off a clever, caustic or downright nasty topper of their own.

And in this fractured cinematic universe that came to me somewhere between the time I dozed off watching David Letterman's year-long late-night victory lap before retirement and my first semi-steaming cup of Folgers this morning, the time line is as bent as my core premise.

So here goes:

First up is Humphrey Bogart's Rick Blaine in "Casablanca" (1942):

"Here's looking at you, kid."

"Get away from me, mister, or I'll call the cops on my iPad. Mommy warned me about guys like you in trench coats. And, once and for all, I'm not interested in the beginning of a beautiful friendship. Oh, and something else, my name's not Louie!" -- 8-year-old walking to the school bus stop.

"I'm going to make him an offer he can't refuse." -- Marlon Brando as Don Vito Corleone in "The Godfather" (1972)

71

"Don't bother, Cotton Cheeks. Whatever offer you make me, Walmart will match it, right there at the register." -- One of those smart, savvy, but slightly annoying coupon-clipping shoppers I seem to always get behind at the checkout counter.

"You talkin' to me?" -- Robert De Niro as Travis Bickle in "Taxi Driver" (1976)

"I sure am, Grandpa. And I have been for 10 minutes. 'Wheel of Fortune' is over and Grandma has gone in the kitchen, so turn down the TV and turn up your hearing aids so I can talk to you. Geez, Grandpa, you never answer my texts. :(" -- Any grandchild in Anytown, USA

"The stuff that dreams are made of." -- Humphrey Bogart as Sam Spade in "The Maltese Falcon" (1941)

"No thank you. We're tourists ... just looking around. It's our first trip to Colorado."

"Wait a minute, wait a minute. You ain't heard nothin' yet!" -- Al Jolson as Jakie Robinowitz in "The Jazz Singer" (1927)

"Yes I did, Grandpa. We all did. If you don't turn up your hearing aids, I'm only going to talk to you on Skype from now on." -- Any grandchild in Anytown, USA :(

"Frankly, my dear, I don't give a damn." -- Clark Gable's Rhett Butler to Vivien Leigh's Scarlett O'Hara in "Gone With the Wind" (1939).

"You think I care, mo#&#@)%&+@&$?" -- Any of about a dozen interchangeable hip-hop rappers spitting out profanities while grabbing their junk.

"You don't understand! I coulda had class. I coulda been a contender. I could've been somebody, instead of a bum, which is what I am." -- Marlon Brando as Terry Malloy in "On the Waterfront" (1954)

"Come on! Hold that double chin up. You're a Kardashian. Be proud. Don't you know you don't have to have talent to be famous? A little plastic surgery will fix that chin, by the way." -- Another Kardashian

MAMA NATURE BEARS DOWN ON 'KUNG FU PANDA 2'

"**L**ord, I know we all have to go sometime. And I've had a fairly decent run, except for the bottom falling out of the film critic profession and all. But please don't let me die at a 'Kung Fu Panda 2' screening.

"Oh God, not a s-s-s-s-sequel!"

These were the frantic thoughts running through my mind last night at the AMC Theater at Northpark on a night when Mother Nature unleashed her own, real adventure-thriller.

Funnel clouds danced across the Dallas-Fort Worth and North Texas sky in concert with wave on wave of wind, heavy rain and -- in some cases -- baseball-size hail.

While the Texas Rangers, Chicago White Sox and fans scurried for cover, Mother Nature stuck mostly to fastballs, although some sliders were reported skidding along streets and back yards.

What started out as just another night of a movie preview screening for me turned into an extended evening of start-and-stop "Kung Fu Panda 2."

I knew what it meant when the lights came up and the noise of heavy rain pounding the theater roof took over audio attention with about 20 minutes remaining in Panda Po's (Jack Black) valiant fight to save ancient China from a determined animated villain (Gary Oldman).

The 3-D glasses were about to come off and the audience was about to be told to abandon the auditorium for the lobby.

So we were and we did. Twice. When the all-clear was finally given, determined "Kung Fu Panda" fans (who stuck it out) and grumbling movie critics (who had no choice) returned for the semi-grand finale.

I must admit, my attention was divided as the final minutes of "Panda 2" unfolded. I had no idea what was going on outside.

"Are any of those funnel clouds in the area touching down, ravaging miles of downtown, businesses, neighborhoods? What about our neighborhood? Are Suellen and Frankie (the doggie) OK? Who's doing better on 'American Idol' tonight, Scotty or Lauren? Why did they kick Haley off, anyway? What if another tornado heads this way?

"Oh God, don't take me out reviewing a cartoon sequel. How could I ever face Gene Siskel, who could write, boy, if I ever get to meet him in Heaven?"

As it turns out, I lived to review movies again. I'm pretty sure my brother, his lady, and his two sons survived the Rangers game ordeal, even though the luck of the draw had them there when all hail broke loose.

And, Suellen and Frankie did just fine at home throughout the scary evening:

"The sirens kept going off and Big Tex (our term for the weather alert voice that blares out of neighborhood speakers) kept telling everyone to take cover," Suellen said.

Not only did they make it through the ordeal, but Suellen grabbed emergency rations and a flashlight and she and Frankie headed for shelter in our safe place, the guest bathroom.

When I got home there were blankets, pillows and Frankie's leash in the bathtub and these emergency rations on the sink:

Two bottles of water, a box of Triscuits and a small can of Del Monte cut green beans.

They never actually got into the bathtub, though. You see, we have a leaky, dripping faucet at the moment.

Survival is one thing, but no one wants to endure waterboarding, even when tornado clouds are playing eenie-meenie-miney-mo overhead.

That would be torture. And one might spill the beans.

MOVIE-MAKING MEMORIES & MORE

"We were driving into Dallas and I started getting that old feeling again," filmmaker, stuntman and all-around great guy Gary Kent said with an old familiar spark in his eye, shortly after we savored a reuniting hug that was too many years coming.

Fate, or possibly pyramid power, brought us together in the early 1970s when Gary and a band of semi-misfits -- actors, actor wannabes, a film-making crew that had amazing faith in a first-time director, scores of people simply curious and more than a few hangers-on -- summoned up all they had to make a feature film titled "The Pyramid."

I was among those mentioned above. I probably fit into several of the categories mentioned. Mostly, though, I wanted to see this beguiling guy named Gary Kent get his movie made (without allowing me to embarrass myself too horribly as one of the cast members).

Gary, his son Chris and Joe O'Connell drove up from Austin on Saturday (Feb. 16, 2013)) to be part of an interview session promoting It Came From Dallas 8 – Behind the 8-Ball fund-raising event put on by the Dallas Producers Association.

O'Connell, a noted film writer (who's been published in The Dallas Morning News and the Austin American-Statesman, just to name a couple newspapers), is making a documentary about Gary's fascinating life and career titled "Love & Other Stunts."

Consider this: The silver-haired Mr. Kent, who lost his wife Tomi (the female lead in "The Pyramid") to cancer and is now facing serious health issues himself, played toughs and bikers in glorious 1960s B-movies like "Satan's Sadists" and "Hell's Angels on

77

Wheels." As a stuntman, Gary doubled big-name stars Jack Nicholson and Robert Vaughan.

When he first got off the bus in Hollywood in 1959, Gary wanted to be the next big movie star. At least he did until he noticed that he wasn't the only determined young new arrival with that idea. In fact, when he noticed that casting agents often tossed bios and publicity photos in the trash before eager young actors even left the room, Gary started looking around for something else to do in the movie industry.

Sometime in the early '60s, Gary Kent got the opening he had been waiting for.

"I was having lunch with someone and they said, 'Jack Nicholson, this young actor, is getting ready to do two Westerns up in Utah, and they're looking for a stuntman.' I said, 'I'm a stuntman,' although I wasn't, of course, but I was going to fake it," Gary said during the Dallas interview.

He first met Nicholson in a small room, that Gary said appeared to be a paper supply room.

"He had a bologna sandwich and he was sitting there. He didn't know anything. I didn't know anything, so we just lied to each other. He said, "We're going up to Utah. Can you take a horse and have it get sick, slow down, fall down and die?' And I said, 'Sure, that's no problem. I can do that,' having no idea what I was going to do."

The Westerns, both directed by Monte Hellman, turned out to be "Ride in the Whirlwind" in 1965 and "The Shooting," which hit silver screens a year later.

That launched Gary's varied career as a stuntman, filmmaker and actor that would bring him to Dallas in the early 1970s. After another film-maker's project failed to make it to that wonderful shout of "Action," Gary decided to write and direct his own film. That project became "The Pyramid," a pyramid-powered, stream-ofconsciousness drama about a TV newsman sick of covering tragic news and looking to find his true center with positive stories.

If "The Pyramid" were released today, it would probably be classified as "realistic fiction," a term that applies to Steven Spielberg's "Lincoln," Ben Affleck's "Argo" and Kathryn Bigelow's "Zero Dark Thirty." That's to say a project based on or inspired by real experiences or events, but Hollywooded-up, so to speak, for the movie-going masses.

A year or so before "The Pyramid" began production in Dallas in the early '70s, I remember seeing Gary's face light up as I told my new friend from Hollywood stories of my own experiences as a television news reporter in the Dallas-Fort Worth market.

Gary -- as all feature filmmakers do -- expanded on what I told him about growing weary of ambulance chasing and reporting on tragedies and scratched out enough funding to add director to his long list of acting and behind-the-scenes credits. He was kind enough to cast me in "The Pyramid," not as the lead TV news reporter (played by the late Charley Brown), but as a television news anchorman.

If you catch the movie trailer on YouTube, you won't see me. But in the frenzied end moments of the trailer, you'll hear me say, "Ladies and gentlemen, please stand by."

Ladies and gentlemen, please stand by Gary Kent.

OH SNAP: I DON'T GET
'WEST SIDE STORY'

T hose who have questioned my comic ability over the years, including me, must at least admit I am in complete harmony in one area with George Carlin, the brilliant late comic uncanny in his ability to observe life.

When it comes to the classic Hollywood musical "West Side Story," the 1961 musical that won 10 Academy Awards including best picture, Carlin didn't and I just don't get it.

What Carlin expressed in the past and what I feel right now is the notion of two bitter rival New York street gangs who hate each other so much that they ... they ... snap their fingers angrily at each other.

Oh the humanity!

Of course the lily white Jets and the Puerto Rican Sharks eventually get around to whipping out their switchblades in this crowd-pleasing rehash of Shakespeare's classic "Romeo and Juliet" yarn. But after all the finger-snapping and high-jumping choreography, though, I share Carlin's take 100 percent:

"I'll cut you, man! But first, let's dance!"

A lady at one of my Movie Memories presentations suggested recently that maybe "West Side Story" is a "chick flick" and guys just don't get it.

That may be the case for some, but I really enjoyed plenty of potentially "chick flickish" musicals. "The Sound of Music" comes to mind, and so does "Oklahoma!" And my disdain for "West Side Story" has nothing to do with all the fighting and hatred.

And I can prove it. My two favorite musicals of all time are "Cabaret" (1972) and "Hedwig and the Angry Inch" *(2001)*, a little ditty about a transsexual punk rocker tormented by the fact that a certain life-altering operation didn't quite work out as planned.

Sorry, but "West Side Story," the movie many consider to be one of the best -- if not the greatest -- musicals of all time just doesn't cut it for me, if you'll excuse the pun.

I wouldn't suggest that you think ill of me for weak puns like that, either, I might just snap my fingers at you with that killer look in my eyes.

RAGING BULL AND 'RAGING BULL'

Thirty-five years ago this month (July, 2015) I got paid to review a movie for the first time.

Reluctantly leaving behind semi-stunned family and friends, I ventured south from the relative comfort and financial security of an enjoyable dead-end job in Dallas to pursue a dream to forge a career as a professional film critic.

Looking back, I'm grateful I landed at the Valley Morning Star, a small daily newspaper in sleepy (at the time) Harlingen, located in far South Texas. The locals and "winter Texans" call it The Valley.

The Valley is not quite Mexico, which my dad used to call Old Mexico, but it's close. Let's put it this way. You don't have to stop at a Texas Border Patrol checkpoint going south on Highway. 281, but you do when you're headed north.

I had what they now call a hidden agenda when I took the lowest-rung job (compiling the scoreboard page) in the sports department at the Valley Morning Star. The world was just waiting for my knowledgeable, witty comments in the world of film criticism. It was just that no one but me realized it at the time, which was 1980. April 1, 1980, in fact.

Yes, I launched the career that has taken me around the U.S. numerous times, to foreign countries including France, Great Britain and Scotland, to the Academy Awards, to a position as film critic for the NBC News Channel and to the Cannes Film Festival (among others) on, uh, April Fools' Day.

Looking back, that explains so much. But to stay focused here, 1980 was a very good year for quality, memorable movies. "The Elephant Man" opened that year, and so did "The Blues Brothers," "Ordinary People" and "The Shining"; you know, the one where a crazed writer played by Jack Nicholson crashes the bathroom door to get to his terrified wife while yelling, "H-E-E-E-E-R-S JOHNNY!"

"Raging Bull," directed by Martin Scorsese and starring Robert De Niro in a brilliant performance as raging boxer-with-issues Jake LaMotta, opened in December that year. In my humble opinion, "Raging Bull" exploded on the screen as the finest film of the decade.

My first review, however, was none of those.

It took me about three months to convince the extremely understanding folks at the Valley Morning Star that what their already fine newspaper needed was a film critic. So on the morning of July 2, I -- with notepad and Mild Duds in hand -- took a seat in a Harlingen movie house to review "Airplane!"

For those who may not be familiar with the wildly comic spoof of every airplane disaster movie (but especially "Zero Hour") that had come before, co-writers and co-directors Jim Abrahams, David Zucker and Jerry Zucker pulled out all the stops from wordplay jokes ("Surely you can't be serious." "I am serious, and don't call me Shirley.") to physical humor like a line of passengers (including a nun with a mean right slap) taking turns to "convince" a hysterical female passenger to get a grip.

I had no idea what the filmmakers and hilarious co-stars Leslie Nielsen, Lloyd Bridges, Robert Hays, Julie Hagerty and Peter Graves were doing, except that it appeared everyone was channeling the Marx Bros. and somehow justifying mayhem and silliness for a new era.

I managed to hold on to my notepad, which examined later was a jumbled mess of wildly drawn lines and OMG! before OMG was cool (if it really is or ever was). It may also be the only time in 35 years of reviewing movies that I ever dropped a Milk Dud.

I realized before the lights even came up that I had a decision to make. "Airplane!" was clearly either a revolutionary new high in lowbrow comedy, or the dumbest movie I had ever seen.

Luckily, I went with both gut feelings. "Airplane!" landed a spot in cinematic history as just that, a cutting-edge dose of lunacy that has inspired scores of imitators.

Recollection of experiences like that and other stops along the path of an entertainment journalist specializing in cinema forged what has become Movie Memories, the public speaking chapter of a life often best lived in the dark.

Mild Duds, anyone?

UNFORTUNATE FILM TITLE
OF THE WEEK

It doesn't matter how entertaining "The Second Best Exotic Marigold Hotel" is, it has already proclaimed itself second best with a most unfortunate movie title.

Sequel or not, what are the geniuses behind the follow-up to the 2011 delightful, poignant tale of British retirees finding adventure in a semi-restored hotel in India thinking?

"How was it?" someone is bound to ask as movie-goers head back out into the daylight after seeing "The Second Best Exotic Marigold Hotel."

"Oh, you know, really semi-top notch, second rate."

What else can they possibly say?

Unfortunate movie titles are nothing new. The action-comic Western "Straight to Hell" didn't set the bar very high in 1986. And there actually was a short film titled "The Bad Movie" in 2004.

Some of you might remember "Really Bad Movie!" on TV a couple of years back. Me? I can't wait for "The Extra Bad Movie," supposedly coming to your neighborhood bijou sometime later this year.

Back in 2007, I interviewed Jerry Seinfeld when he stopped off in Dallas to stir up a little buzz, if you will, for "Bee Movie." The legendary TV sitcom star told me he came up with the idea for the computer-animated tale of a bee with a mind of his own during a lull in dinner conversation with Steven Spielberg.

You may remember that Seinfeld voiced the lead character, Barry B. Benson, himself. It was a labor of love for Seinfeld, who spent about four years getting the project to the screen.

But I remember thinking there was something unfortunate about that title: "Bee Movie."

So I took a deep breath, decided why not challenge one of the great comic minds of our generation and said something like, "You know, to some people that term B-movie means second rate or low budget."

Seinfeld looked at me a little funny and said, "You're the first person who has brought that up."

Not that there's anything wrong with that.

SPRINGING A WIKI LEAK:
THE ROYAL WEDDING TIMELINE

A man's home is his castle. *In Great Britain, thanks to the Royals, that can literally be the case.*
If you ask me, every bride and groom should launch a happy marriage in a 13th century tomb (Westminster Abbey), share a ceremonial first wedded kiss in front of thousands of adoring subjects and ... wait for it ... squint skyward for not one, but two flyovers to celebrate the very special day.

I've got to admit that beats a wedding in someone's back yard converted into a wedding gazebo, a wedding singer so bad I still can't get the sight of my soon-to-be step-son grimacing and one of my best friends poking fingers into his ears in a vain attempt to shield himself from the off-key warbling.

But enough about my wedding. Let's get on to the new Royal Coupling.

That would be last Friday's (April 9, 2011) blissful union of the UK's Prince William and Kate Middleton, a so-called commoner.

Or, perhaps it's more appropriate to call it the blissful reunion of Willy and Kate since the couple have allegedly been, shall we say, royally shacking up since eight months before the engagement was even announced.

Word is that the Archbishop of York, no less, "gave his backing" to the shacking.

Party on, Brits.

At first, I was among those who questioned why all the U.S. news agencies went gaga -- not Lady Gaga, just gaga -- over Friday's nuptial festivities. Some network anchors and reporters (mostly women, I'm relieved to report) even purchased and sported brightly colored hats they can never even think of using for anything else for the occasion.

Gradually, I came around to the notion of embracing, out of curiosity, mind you, something I couldn't escape anyway.

If you question this theory, may I remind you that all of this country's big-time network TV anchor throats (announcers) were caught way away from their posts and red-faced when a marauding tornado the size of Kirstie Alley when she's off her diet did its best to wipe Alabama off the map hours before a British bride and groom (who chooses not to sport a wedding band) vowed up.

At least Wiki leaks is on top of things. Here, then, is the just-exposed royal timeline of last Friday's day of days:

8 a.m.: Prince William (the balding one) is given the new title of the Duke of Cambridge by his grandmother, the queen, to mark his marriage to Kate Middleton.

10:13: Prince William, wearing a red tunic of an Irish Guards officer, leaves Clarence House in a chauffeur-driven Bentley with his brother, Prince Harry. Harry sports a Blues and Royals officer's uniform after deciding at the last minute against the Nazi uniform he wore to a Halloween party a couple of years back.

10:18: The princes arrive at Westminster Abbey to rapturous applause and cheers from fans. Only a few yell out, "Yo, Harry, where's the Nazi uniform?"

10:47: The queen and Duke of Edinburgh arrive at Westminster Abbey in a Rolls-Royce limousine. The Queen Mum's dressed in a primrose dress with matching hat and coat. The Duke doses off in a military uniform.

11:00: The bride arrives right on time. She's wearing a gown with lace applique floral detail designed by Sarah Burton from the House of Ross Dress for Less.

11:20: There's a fancy wedding ... yada, yada, yada.

12:28 p.m.: The newlyweds arrive at Buckingham Palace where William is overheard telling Harry, "I've got to visit the other royal throne, if you know what I mean, Bro."

1:27: William and Kate kiss for the first time as hubby and The Missus on the balcony of Buckingham Palace as hundreds of thousands cheer down below (outside the royal gates, of course). NBC, which had been counting down the seconds as if the royal smooch were the launching of the space shuttle, is busy gabbing about something else and misses the money shot. (Somewhere back in Plano, Texas, USA a lone writer marks this glaring NBC flub as the high point of his day. "Yes!")

1:35: Royal lunch is served. Beans and bangers (weenies). Again.

2:17: The queen excuses herself to catch the afternoon soaps on the telly. Alone for the first moment as husband and wife, Prince Willy suggests to Kate that it's time for a little graby-graby to celebrate the royal union. One of the servants Kate and William said they'd do without thought she heard this from behind a door: "Forget it, bub. I'm not about to ruin my wedding day with heathen relations, royal or not."

2:18: Royal sulking.

3:12: A deep sigh is heard though the keyhole of William and Kate's chambers, then the sound of a TV remote clicking into action.

3:13 to 5:45: The newly crowned Duke of Cambridge spends the late afternoon alone watching a cricket match between Kent and Middlesex. If you'll forgive a royal pun, Middlesex doesn't score either.

AT THE MOVIES: 2025

L et's begin our not-too-distant future visit to the neighborhood movie gigaplex in the parking lot.

What's a gigaplex?

Oh you silly people still stuck in the early 21st century. Movie gigaplexes have 100 screens, of course.

Now, back to the parking lot. No need to worry about how far away from the building you park. That's so old learning dome. The theater will send a personal pod for you and your guests. Just find a parking space, glance at the button on the dash marked PI (Plug in), and your car will be all charged up when the pod returns you.

I like the pods. Just take two or three steps from your car into the pod and those are the last steps you need to take before you return to your car.

That's right, no stopping at the ticket booth, concession stand or even, ahem, the restroom. All of that is taken care of right there in the pod, which, when landed and locked-in-place, becomes your couch-away-from-couch. I don't want to say too much about how the restroom-stop problem has been solved. Just know this, catheters will soon be greatly improved.

And did I mention that movies are pet friendly now? Sure, bring Astro along. Each pod comes with invisible sound mufflers so your dog -- or dogs for those so-minded -- can enjoy popular movies like "Guardians of the Galaxy: Yet Another Sequel" or Richard Linklater's eclectic favorite "Grandpahood" right along with the family. It's all included with any $109.99 adult ticket. That's only $107.99 for seniors, children under 3 and military (Our side only, please).

Once your pod is locked and loaded, concessions like Blast Off, the instant energy caffeine drink equal to three full pots of coffee, or

Milk Duds arrive in your armrest automatically. Yes, Milk Duds are still around but they now come in three varieties: Melt in Your Mouth, Extra-Soft or Regular, still the favorite movie candy of dentists everywhere.

Oh, here's a couple of things a little different than they used to be at the movies. Talking is encouraged. In fact, the louder the better. Most people shout out how many likes they have on Bodybook (It's about so much more than just the Face these days).

And wristcomms -- once called cellphones -- are left on at all times in movie houses now. That announcement comes right after President Bieber's safe driving plea to drivers 11 and younger and Vice President Jenna Bush Hager's "Previews of Coming Tweets."

Goody, that includes "Social Media." That's what we've come to see.

The 200-by-90-foot screen is filled with Tweets from us, you, the neighbors, celebrities (including any, let's just say, risqué photos they tried to protect, but couldn't), world leaders and drone pilots safely ensconced on leather sofas in Washington bunkers bombing the heck out of undesirables (definition to come when President Bieber and his cabinet figure it out).

This is so much more fun now that privacy rules have been voted out by the TMZ-controlled Congress. People can now post whatever they like and it's out there for the world to see. Of course the fact that due to worldwide giga-use Twitter now limits each tweet to six digits, there is a bit of sameness to the futuristic movie-going experience.

As a theater full of people scream out their Bodybook like totals and wristcomms light up the auditorium enough for me to see the corpse-like pallor on hundreds of chubby faces slurping down caffeine and inhaling Milk Duds, here's what I'm looking at on a giant movie screen:

Wh up? N much ... Wh up? N much ... Wh up? N much ... Wh up? N much ... Wh up? N much ... Wh up? N much ... Wh up? N much ... Wh up? N much ... Wh up? N much ...

Sweet.

R.I.P.: O'TOOLE, FONTAINE, 'BILLY JACK'

The grim reaper has been busy over the past few days.

A cinematic icon, an Oscar-winning actress and one of Hollywood's legendary rule-breakers all died between Thursday and Sunday (Dec. 12-15, 2013).

The loss of Peter O'Toole, an eight-time Academy Award nominee widely known as the star of "Lawrence of Arabia," hit me the hardest. O'Toole passed away at the age of 81 Saturday, after announcing his retirement from acting in July, 2012.

Hollywood also lost two other notables. Joan Fontaine, younger sister of Academy Award-winner Olivia de Havilland, died Sunday.

A casting favorite of Alfred Hitchcock in films like "Suspicion" and "Rebecca," Fontaine was 96.

Finally, Tom Laughlin may not exactly be a household name these days. But as Billy Jack, the tough-as-nails ex-Green Beret of 50-50 Native American and White Man ancestry, Laughlin took it to "the man," and protected students of an arts school in "Billy Jack," the early '70s action-drama he starred in, directed, co-wrote (with co-star Delores Taylor) and pretty much self-marketed to widespread appeal.

Laughlin, who succumbed to complications of pneumonia, died Thursday at the age of 82.

O'Toole's death hit me the hardest, though, and not just because the "unrepentant hell raiser" (according to published reports) commanded the most marquee power.

I never met the star of "Becket," "The Lion in Winter," "Goodbye Mr. Chips" (1971), "The Ruling Class," "My Favorite

Year" or "The Stunt Man" face-to-face. I was lucky enough to have a telephone conversation with O'Toole in 1988, however.

I was nervous. O'Toole, most likely spending an excruciating two or three-hour block of time on the telephone with a seemingly never-ending list of film critics to promote a so-so at best fantasy comic-horror titled "High Spirits," was obviously bored and distant by the time we spoke.

In fact, the acting legend did very little to mask his boredom as we chatted and he said all the right things about a movie he had probably already filed away as minor at best.

And you know what? I couldn't have cared less. Through the wonder of telephone communication, I was speaking to T.E. Lawrence (of Arabia), King Henry II ("Becket"), Arthur Chipping ("Goodbye, Mr. Chips"), and, my personal favorite, Alan Swann of the raucous 1982 comedy "My Favorite Year."

Directed by Richard Benjamin, "My Favorite Year" features O'Toole as an Errol Flynn-like movie star with a serious drinking problem who agrees to be the featured guest star on a popular U.S. variety TV show. Swann panics, though, when he learns he'll be appearing in front of a live audience.

As Swann, O'Toole spouts one of my favorite movie lines of all time:

"I'm not an actor. I'm a movie star!"

Rest in peace, Mr. O'Toole.

And just for the record: Yes you are, and I'll always remember you as one of the finest actors ever to grace the silver screen.

REMEMBERING ROCKIN' ROBIN

"**N**o words."

That's all Billy Crystal, Robin Williams' good friend and fellow acclaimed comic performer, could Tweet Aug. 11, 2014 as word of Williams death, an "apparent suicide" according to news reports, spread with the same raging fire that propelled a comic genius -- yes, a genius -- to world stardom and, apparently, unbearable depths of depression.

I have words, a few at least, to say or, more correctly, to expel from my deeply saddened state. Perhaps they might, if only a little, ease some of the kick-in-the-gut sting felt by Williams' survivors. That includes family and friends, of course, but also anyone, including this scribe, who smiles when he or she hears the bellowed phrase "Good m-o-r-n-i-n-g Vietnam!" or conjures up the image of "Mrs. Doubtfire" (Williams in drag) setting her breasts on fire in the kitchen.

I knew Robin Williams about as well as any road warrior film critic who, over three decades or so, sat down with the almost always manic comic tsunami for short spurts at a time to discuss his latest movie.

Often, the interviews would be what's known in the industry as "round-table" interviews. Five, six or seven film critics or entertainment reporters sit around a round table in a hotel suite usually in Los Angeles or New York. The "talent" enters the room and takes the empty chair at the table and chats up the movie for 30 to 40 minutes; responding to mostly softball questions.

On one occasion, which looking back might have been one of Williams' tough days in his continuing battle against substance abuse and/or depression, the master rapid-fire comedian was, let's just say, melancholy.

In a situation where press members around a table often have to verbally joust to get their question in, moments of silence were creeping in between questions to Williams. I found myself sitting right next to Williams that day. He was fighting the good fight to keep the banter coming, which obviously most of my fellow journalists expected. But Robin Williams just wasn't feeling it that day.

"Carpe Diem. Seize the day, boys," Williams said as college professor John Keating in his Oscar-nominated performance in "Dead Poets Society" in 1989.

So I did. I asked Williams where his rapid-fire comic one-liners come from and how they ignite.

"I don't really know," he said quietly. "It's almost like my head opens up and my brain is an antenna. Signals from outer-space fill my brain. I just let them out."

And let them out, he did. Brilliantly, in fact, for a lot of years.

Laughing on the outside/crying on the inside. That classic description of a clown is too trite and too simple to explain the high highs, the low lows and the inner turmoil that Williams must have been channeling, along with his ongoing battle with horned demons of alcohol and substance abuse.

Some words: You left us, Robin, for reasons we may never know but you, obviously, knew all too well. Many of us, including your peers like Billy Crystal and Steve Martin, are stunned and speechless. All I can say is that you left a very deep imprint on this place you have recently departed.

R.I.P.: Rockin' Robin.

YATES INSPIRED MY BREAK AWAY
TO FILM CRITICISM

Four-time Oscar-nominated British director Peter Yates has died.

Yates passed (Jan. 9, 2011) in London at 82 after suffering a long illness, according to British newspaper website guardian.co.uk.

Serious movie lovers will remember Yates as the director who guided Steve McQueen through "Bullitt" in 1968. Together, with McQueen doing much of his own driving, according to the Guardian article, Yates and McQueen catapulted movie chase scenes to a new, dangerous, higher level.

As director, Yates was nominated twice for Academy Awards; for "The Dresser" in 1983 and for "Breaking Away" in 1979.

I liked "Bullitt" and I appreciated "The Dresser," a compelling backstage drama starring Albert Finney and Tom Courtenay.

"Breaking Away," however, changed my life path.

In 1979, when "Breaking Away" debuted, I was prepping for a career as a movie critic. I had a job; a good paying one, in fact, as a bartender in Dallas.

I never intended to tend bar, really. But I had hopped off my career path as a television news anchor a few years earlier to make the world laugh as a stand-up comedian.

Great comedy comes from suffering, the big boys said, so I toiled away as a cab driver, a waiter, a bar manager and finally a bartender. I found out pretty quickly that the world -- or at least as many people as I encountered -- preferred to laugh at me as a TV news person.

As a comedian? Not so much.

So I morphed (way ahead of my time, I might point out) to Plan B: Professional movie critic. I won't bore you with too many details here. Let's just say that while I was searching for a newspaper that would have me, I cut back my bartending to four nights a week.

The plan was to see three movies a week and then sit down and write reviews of them. That's a practice I recommend to aspiring film critics to this day.

One dreary afternoon in 1979, I wandered into Dallas's Highland Park Village theater for a film I knew nothing about titled "Breaking Away." Some might call it merely a stylish bicycle race drama with some comedy.

They would be wrong, though. What Yates did with "Breaking Away" was deftly construct a portrait of restless blue-collar American youth of Bloomington, Ind. taking on those better off financially in a relay bicycle race that amounted to a clash of class titans.

Jackie Earle Haley, San Antonio's Oscar nominee for "Little Children" in 2006, played Moocher, one of the "cutters" (locals). But that's not the reason "Breaking Away" and Yates' direction have left such a mark on my professional psyche.

When I went to afternoon movies in the late '70s, I seemed to always share a half (or less) empty auditorium with well-dressed businessmen (salesmen, I'm guessing) who, for whatever reason, were shucking their professional duties of the day.

They were a tough movie-watching bunch to excite. But at the end of "Breaking Away," when the race neared the finish line, I saw grown men -- perhaps "cutters" themselves at one time -- stand up and applaud and cheer.

That, my friends, is about all you can ask of a filmmaker.

I was so inspired that I amped up my courage to make it as a film critic despite long odds.

So, thank you, Peter Yates. Although I never got a chance to thank you in person, I won't forget the filmmaker who inspired me to shift gears out of a comfort zone and race on to my life's calling.

Rest in peace.

BLOG, BLAH, BLAH

With apologies to noted 17th century philosopher René Descartes:

I blog, therefore I think I am.

In ancient times, I don't know three or four years ago, we didn't blog.

We kept our idiotic, self-serving thoughts to ourselves. Unless, of course, we inserted one of those four page, single-spaced nausea-inducing Family Newsletter updates into our Christmas cards. Excuse me, holiday cards.

For the most part, we – make that I – refrained from solving all the world's problems and unleashing uneducated or unproven thoughts on others.

If you didn't receive my recent blog titled "You Have No Right To Send Your Every Waking Thought/Pot Pie Recipe To My Inbox," send me your e-mail address and I'll shoot it right back to you.

We learned recently that there was trouble on the Space Station. It seems something knocked out the main computers, which, by the way, were the Russians' part of the joint space venture. I'm not surprised. And you shouldn't be either, especially if you paid attention to my May, 2005 blog "Maybe One of the Space Station Computer Systems Should Be American Made – Dell's Got Some Doozies."

Didn't get it? Not a problem. Stop what you're doing right now and send me an e-mail. I'll shoot a copy right back at 'cha.

A very learned man, I think it was the late Don Ho (TheLateDonHo.org), said one time that every single byte of information generated electronically never really disappears. They just float off into the atmosphere.

That, I'm pretty sure, is what took out the Space Station computers. All the pot pie recipes, "American Idol" votes, music downloads, cellular telephone conversations (many about pot pies) and Britney Spears photos showing her getting out of a limo jammed the unreliable Russian computer hard drives on the Space Station.

So give the constant blogging a rest, people. Our space system – the link to the final frontier – might just depend on it.

Before I forget it, if you're the last person on earth who hasn't seen the Britney Spears photos, you must have deleted my "Oh No You Didn't, Britney" blog by mistake. Not to worry, I forgive you.

Drop me an email and I'll shoot another copy right back to you.

Of course you can also go to my website, StopTheWorldIWantToGrabACafeLatte.fr. You'll find the "Oh No You Didn't, Britney" link on the Paris/Britney/Me and Other Fascinating People page.

While you're at my website, you'll want to reread the fun blogs "All the Movies Chevy Chase Barfed In" and "Grabbing a Secret Smoke with Obama" (subtitled "Out Back with Barack"). They'll be a hoot to revisit, even though I'm pretty sure you've seen them. I hired a guy in New Jersey to spam them to every computer on the planet six or seven times a day. Of course, I also had him pay special attention to our friends on the Space Station. He sent them constantly to our brave astronauts, cosmonauts and people so filthy rich they ride space shuttles like we splurge for dessert after our all-you-can-eat buffet dinner. (Get there before 5 and save 50 cents. Don't tell them where you heard it, though.)

By the way, if you can't get through to StopTheWorldIWantToGrabACafeLatte.fr right away, please keep trying. It's not that busy, really. But I spend seven or eight hours a day clicking constantly on it myself. I need the hits. Got to keep up, you know.

A few million more and I can charge for advertising. But you know that. You must have read it in my "How to Trick Some Suckers Into Advertising on Your Website" blog.

Didn't get that one? You know the drill.

I'll be waiting right here.

BOOMERS SOONER, BOOMERS LATER

R eady for some very good news for mature movie-goers? Long virtually ignored and pretty much scorned by Hollywood and filmmakers, baby boomers are suddenly the new darlings of the movie multiplex.

Why? Because seniors who cut their cinematic appreciation teeth on everything from "Some Like It Hot" (1959) to "Star Wars" (1977), learned early to appreciate the magic of movies in a movie theater.

I'm not too crazy about the headline The Hollywood Reporter put on its fine article on the subject, but under the headline "Old People, Old Stars: Hollywood's New Hot Demo Is Saving the Box Office" lies redemption in print for us Boomers. We've spent too many years watching Hollywood bow down to 18-to-24-year-old iPhone wielding, texting customers who only demand the latest comic book hero or romanticized moody young vampire up on a movie screen.

Finally, Hollywood bean counters have noticed plus-50 patrons lining up for adult-themed movies like "Hope Springs," the stale marriage revamp comic-drama starring Meryl Streep and Tommy Lee Jones, and even the muscle-flexing actioner "The Expendables 2" starring 66-year-old Sylvester Stallone and '80s action heroes Chuck Norris, Jean-Claude Van Damme and even ex-California guv Arnold Schwarzenegger.

"After years of fawning over the fanboy, Hollywood is suddenly embracing the boomer, who is turning out to be the most avid moviegoer of all as teenagers and young adults disappear behind video game consoles, computers and iPhones. 'It's the next frontier. Younger people have pretty much been milked,' says Bill Newcott, entertainment editor at AARP's The Magazine," proclaimed The Hollywood Reporter article.

The article itself provides the numbers: There were 78 million or so baby boomers around in 2010, and that number is growing.

Here's the why Hollywood is finally listening. We love movies. Many of us can remember when Saturday afternoon at the movies meant a newsreel, coming attractions, a cartoon, a double-feature and a 10 cent or quarter (depending on which end of the baby boomer spectrum we fall into) telephone call to mom:

"Come get us Mom, we're through."

We weren't through, though. That appreciation of something magical happening on that big lighted wall at the front of the room ignited in our formative years never faded away. We shared it with girlfriends and boyfriends, moms and dads, buddies from the block and strangers.

When something really special happened on the screen and the light faded and the house lights came on, we somehow exited the movie house closer -- bonded somehow -- than when we entered with a box of popcorn in one hand and a soft drink and maybe even a giant dill pickle in the other.

From this aisle seat, a message. Dear semi-interested young movie-goers who simply must check text messages every 30 seconds while disrupting everyone else in the auditorium:

We are the baby boomers and we want our movie theaters back.

We will watch in awe when something spectacular happens. We will cheer the heroes -- yes, even those actors who are now card-carrying AARP members -- and go on the intended weepy-eyed emotional roller coaster ride when love goes wrong or a miracle happens and things end well.

And we will eat our popcorn just like we always have, except for those of us with digestive challenges. And we'll revel in the splendor of Milk Duds, except for those of us with dental issues in danger of losing a crown.

And if our iPhone rings (Yes, rings!), it won't be because we simply must text. It'll be because we can't remember how to turn the darn thing off.

OLD YEAR'S RESOLUTIONS

It took me a while, decades in fact, but I've finally gotten a little smarter about New Year's resolutions.

I'm not making them anymore.

Instead, this year, I'm going back to make right on some busted resolutions from my past.

Age 7 (1954) -- After an unfortunate and soul-crushing accident while asleep and spending the night at a friend's house across the street from Granny and Wally's (grandparents), I vowed that New Year 1954 would be the year that I would never wet the bed again.

That one worked itself out, thanks, I suppose, to aging a little. Or, come to think of it, it might have had something to do with cutting down on giant Fizzies drinks shortly before bedtime.

Remember Fizzies, those giant candy pills that we plopped into a glasses of water to make our own soft drinks in the '50s and '60s? Well, don't tell your kids or grandchildren, but Fizzies are back. (If the kids are coming over and Fizzies are on the menu, do yourself a favor and dig out the plastic sheets.)

Age 12 (1959) -- All the kids I admired on TV in the 1950s like Ricky Nelson ("The Adventures of Ozzie & Harriet"), Tommy Kirk ("Mickey Mouse Club") and Jerry Mathers ("Leave It To Beaver") were slim. Naturally, I assumed that I was too, especially since my older brother fit the sleek-build profile.

Imagine my horror, then, when my mother, who always made sure my brother and I started each new school year off with a new pair of Levi's and shoes, marched me into the Penney's Boys Department.

Someone could probably ram a hot metal rod though my brain without erasing the self-esteem-crushing memory of what the salesman told my mom:

"Well, we'll need to take this young man over to the Husky Boys section of Levi's."

That word "husky," which I still hate, hit me like a lightning bolt. I clearly heard what the Demon From Hell (Opinions stated by this writer do, indeed, reflect the opinions of this publication) Penney's sales clerk said to my Mother.

When it settled uneasily into my rattled psyche, however, it was recorded to last until the end of time (way past when the Mayans shut everything down in mid-December) thusly:

"Would you like me to just take him out back and put him out of his misery now, or would you prefer to subject him to a lifetime of struggling to zip up his jackets because the zipper fasteners will forever be out of sight below his bulging belly?"

Mom opted to let me live, and I determined in 1959 to fight my way out of the Husky Dept. It took some time. If you catch me in a good place on my lifelong yo-yo weight cycle, though, I'm out of the husky (now, thankfully called "relaxed fit") section, at least until the next predictable relapse.

Predictable? Yeah-huh. It almost always coincides with a week-long sale of Blue Bell Ice Cream at 10 pints for $10. Addiction is a brutal mistress, but I can control even that when I grit my teeth and concentrate.

All I have to do is recall the painful sound of my stiff new Levi Husky Jeans rubbing together between my legs and making an ear-piercing (to me, at least) "swish, swish" sound as I walked the shiny, freshly waxed halls of Robert E. Lee Junior High School in Grand Prairie, Texas.

Lunch cost 35 cents back then. Some of us decked out in Levi's Huskies as our teen years loomed dead ahead and the 1950s were about to bow out in favor of the gritty '60s remember that an ice cream bar only cost a nickel in the lunchroom.

At least one of us recalls that when Mistress Sweet Tooth had us firmly in her grisly grasp, you could get right (until guilt took over) with seven Fudgesicles for that 35 cents.

THE TRIP TO BOUNTIFUL, TOO

As the brakes on the bus that isn't really a bus whoosh, the driver -- a calming soul with a Chicago Bulls cap pulled down low over his ears -- says, "OK, folks, just one more pick up."

The doors open and Jonathan Winters, looking to be in his mid-30s and grinning from ear to ear, bounds up the steps. "Man, this is the best I've felt my entire life," Winters blurts.

"Your entire what," a serious, but polite and slightly giddy British woman replies.

"Hey, you look like ... you *are* Margaret Thatcher," Winters almost shouts. "And isn't that Annette Funicello across the aisle? I remember her. She looks great, in fact young and energetic enough to put those Mickey Mouse Club ears back on. Say, what's going on here?"

"You'll understand soon, Mr. Winters. Just relax and rest assured that we're off to someplace wonderful and without prejudices of any kind. There will be no such thing as liberals or conservatives, racial tension or even pain and suffering."

(Thatcher, with a knowing smile, nods in the direction of a woman a few seats away.) "Isn't that right?"

"Right you are, ma'am."

"Please forgive me," Winters says to the other woman, "but I don't recognize you."

"Call me Casino Sue, Mr. Winters. I've been a fan of yours since I saw you do that Maude Frickert routine on 'The Tonight Show' way back when Johnny Carson was host. You were one funny lady. I mean ... well, you know what I mean."

"Of course, Sue. Thanks," Winters responds.

"Hey, Maggie. May I call you Maggie, Mrs. Thatcher?"

"If you don't mind, Mr. Winters, Margaret will do."

"Sorry, ma'am. Of course. I meant no disrespect. Hey, Maggie ... just kidding, loosen up a little, who's that guy hunched over that iPhone up in front of us?"

"That's Roger Ebert," Thatcher replies. "He's been trying to send a text message to his wife and Tweets to his thousands of followers the whole trip."

Ebert scratches out a quick note and hands it to Thatcher: "I have 600,000 online friends and fans who count on me. I can't reach them."

"You've already reached them, Roger, and you'll always be in their hearts. Don't worry, you won't be forgotten. As for Chaz, your loving wife and helpmate will join you sooner than you can imagine," Thatcher says.

"Excuse me, Roger, but why are you writing notes anyway?" Winters asks.

"I lost my voice years ago in a horrible bout with cancer," Ebert says. "I can't speak."

"Well, you just did, bub," Winters replies with his impeccable comic timing.

"I did, didn't I?" Ebert beams, looking like he did in his heyday.

"You sure did, Roger," the bus driver says calmly as he turns around and removes his Bulls cap.

"Gene ... Gene Siskel! You old son-of-a-gun," Roger shouts. "Great to see you! But don't you need to keep your hands on the wheel?"

"I'm not really driving this bus, Roger. I just like to keep two thumbs up there on the wheel for old times' sake."

"Say, are we there yet? How long will this trip take, anyway," Winters asks.

"Do you want to tell him or should I?" Siskel asks his passengers.

In unison, Margaret Thatcher, Roger Ebert, Annette Funicello, Jack Pardee, Bonnie Franklin and Casino Sue (Taylor) say, "A blink of an eye."

SOME OF THE NEWS
THAT'S FIT TO PRINT

T he word curmudgeon is pathetically inadequate to describe near-legendary Dallas broadcaster Alex Burton, who died Thursday (Sept. 13, 2012) in Dallas at the age of 80.

Yet you're bound to hear Burton lovingly described that way, as an iconoclast who could sometimes come across as a grump.

True, the Alex I knew back in the 1970s was curious, persistent and aggressive. Let's just say he preferred to poke a stick into a hornet's nest to idly walking by.

Back then, when I was a wide-eyed cub TV reporter in the sprawling Dallas-Fort Worth market, we looked up to Burton because he didn't flaunt his extensive experience, his razor-sharp wit or his fearlessness when tough questions needed to be asked.

We called Alex Burton something other than curmudgeon back then. We called him a newsman.

Look around. No, really look around. How many of the golden throats, entertainment-slanted news readers or barely adequate TV news personalities can we truly refer to as newsmen (or women) today?

Alex Burton was one. A damn good one.

Read Burton's obit and you'll be reminded (or informed if you don't already know) that he once drew long-lasting notoriety by conversing with a plant he named "Arthur" while putting his unique spin on the midnight news at WBAP-TV (now KXAS-TV) in the '60s.

Joe Simnacher describes Alex quite well in the Dallas Morning News obituary:

"An adaptable survivor of ever-changing radio and television formats, he had a long and diverse career as a reporter, narrator, pundit and general observer of the human condition."

I was lucky enough to have Alex observe my human condition a few times in the 1970s. Early in the decade, while I prowled the streets as a news reporter for KTVT-TV, Alex and I, along with a few other brave (No, make that suckered-in) TV and radio types, volunteered to serve as guinea pigs for a public service experiment to show the dangers of driving under the influence.

It may be difficult to believe today, but we actually were given a shot of whiskey every 30 minutes. Then, we would get behind the wheel of a car (on a semi-carefully monitored closed course) to see how well we could navigate around traffic cones.

There is no way something like this would happen today. But cameras were rolling as we downed shots, then downed innocent traffic cones. Several things were discovered during that long, increasingly blurry afternoon. (1) Drinking and driving is a seriously dangerous no-no. (2) It is possible to continue driving an automobile for a while, anyway, with three of those bright orange cones lodged between the bumper and wheel.

And (3): It's a lot easier to sing loud and proud in public when you've had a few.

Somewhere -- probably out in the garage aging badly (not unlike your friendly scribe) -- is a photo that ran in either the now-defunct Dallas Times Herald or the Dallas Morning News of Alex Burton, yours truly, and a couple other DFW reporters howling at the moon at the conclusion of the event that seems to have happened only yesterday.

In the late '70s, Alex showed how compassionate, loyal or perhaps desperate for guests on his afternoon KRLD radio talk show he could be.

At the time, I was chasing a dream to be this country's next comedy sensation. Chevy Chase won that race, but that's not why I called this meeting.

I was about a third of the comedy duo Ratso & Lulu. We had attracted a little notoriety of our own around town, so Alex invited us to be guests for an hour (I think) on his show. Lulu was very funny, so I pretty much kept my trap shut and let her and Alex work. I never was as funny as I wanted to be verbally. Having studied the comic greats, however, I knew enough to know why George Burns remained silent and puffed away on his cigar and let Gracie Allen do the heavy comic lifting.

Alex conducted that interview like he was waving a baton in front of the New York Philharmonic: accenting things when needed or just letting the music (comedy, in this case) swell to some pretty darn memorable crescendos.

Rest in peace, Alex. Thanks for all the guidance and kindness you showed me and I'm sure many others like me.

And, oh yeah, tell the moon I said hello.

Made in the USA
Columbia, SC
06 September 2019